Living a Wealthy Life

Stories of Developing an Abundance in All Five Forms of Wealth

Diau,

May you have a successful 2018 & Beyond.

KAC PATEL
3.1.2018

Contents

I Believe I Am Rich

I was born in Phoenix, North Carolina on August 24, 1914. My grandmother, Anna Jane Hall, was a freed slave. My mother, Louisa Anna Hall was very young when I was born, so my grandmother raised me. The sun rose and set on my grandmother in my eyes. She taught me at a very early age to pray and have faith because life was not always fair, but we had to strive for the best despite any obstacles in our path. The obstacles at that time were Jim Crow.

There were two experiences in my childhood that taught me life lessons that would shape my life, and that I would share with my children and grandchildren. I remember how proud I was of finally being able to go to school. My mother and grandmother made a big deal of it. I didn't understand segregation at the time. I was just happy to be in our one room school.

When I got my report card, I ran home as quickly as I could and gave it to my grandmother. Most African-Americans at that time could not read, and my mother and grandmother were no different. We had a neighbor, Aunt Sara, who could read, so my mother told me to take to her so she could read it to me. I was so excited I skipped to her house and handed her my report card. As I anxiously waited, I saw a frown on her face and she said to me, "Don't you ever bring me a report card like this again."

I laugh about it now but I was very disappointed. Aunt Sara told me to read everything I could get my hands on, and so I did just that. The joy of reading opened a brand-new world for me. My most read book, of course, is my Bible.

This is something that I in turn shared with my children. I express to all of them, my grands and great grands, it is important to get your education. No one can ever take that from you. It is crucial to empower the mind. I would go to the

Salvation Army and buy books for all of them. I am proud to say that we have high school graduates, college graduates, teachers, nurses and business owners in our family.

It was not easy as the world was very unfriendly for black people, but we are all a part of God's family. I wanted my family to know that they were great because they were children of God, no matter what any man says.

Life is like a bed of roses, there is beauty amidst the thorns. While I was growing up, there was not much work for women, especially black women. I remember my grandmother would grow peanuts and she would give me my own to sell. I would sell my peanuts and have my own money. I was so proud of myself and wanted to buy a Coca Cola and some cookies. At that time, blacks were not allowed to buy a Coca Cola and could be killed for having one. You see, it was assumed you had stolen it. So, cookies it was, and save the rest. My grandmother taught me the value of a dollar. You never spend it all if you can help it; you always save for a rainy day. I learned that if you cannot find a job, you create one.

I am now 102 years old, and have seen many things. I still love to read and always manage to save a dollar. Reading is hard now, but I have books on tape that I listen to. I have seen Barack Obama become president, and who would have thought I would see that in my lifetime? People treat me like a celebrity, they can't believe I am my age. I am a just an old lady that loves people, especially my family.

I have always worked hard and never had much money. With God's grace, I have always had my needs met. If you want to know, I believe I am a rich person. Rich with love and family. My children and my grands and their children show me so much love, and as I reflect on them they are like flowers, scattered all over the place.

~ Christine E. Adams   April 13, 2017

* * * * *

My grandmother was beautiful, inside and out. She taught me much about the duality of life. She loved all her children, grandchildren, and great grandchildren – she even lived to see a great, great grandchild. Once my grandmother got to know you, you were her child and she loved you, too. She had enough love in her heart for everyone. Even with all she lived through, she was carefree and loved life. The difficult times for her didn't linger; they were just flickers of memory. She taught us all to be grateful in all things, and she was my rock. I miss her.

~ Yvette Adams   August 12, 2017

* * * * *

Christine E. Adams

1914 - 2017

* * * * *

Introduction

Wealth isn't what you think.

Or, rather, it may not be what you have been led to believe. Many people, when they think of wealth, only have a picture of having a lot of money. There is no doubt that money IS a part of wealth. But, are all people who have a lot of money wealthy? The answer isn't as obvious as you might think.

Consider this. If someone has a lot of money, but has no discretionary time to enjoy it, are they really wealthy? Is the person who works 80 or more hours a week, and has little time for anything else, really wealthy?

If a person earns a lot of money, but hates what they do to earn the money, are they really wealthy? It is probably better to be miserable in your circumstances and have money, than to be miserable and broke. But, miserable people aren't really wealthy, no matter how much money they have.

Imagine a person who is so out of shape that they have trouble walking up a flight of stairs. Are they wealthy? Would you consider a multi-millionaire who has a life-threatening physical condition to be wealthy? How about the person who has ALS – commonly known as Lou Gehrig's disease? Even if they were on the Forbes 400 list, are they truly wealthy?

Finally, imagine a person who runs a successful company and who earns seven figures plus in a year. This person drives a brand-new Mercedes, lives in a 10,000 square foot mansion, has a pool boy and a live-in maid. At first glance, would you think that that person is wealthy? Now, what if you learned that this person with a lot of money is twice divorced, estranged from their children and has no real friends. Even with that income and outward signs of financial wealth, is that really a wealthy life?

Don't misunderstand. There is absolutely nothing wrong with wanting to make a lot of money. Nothing will take the place of money in the arena in which it is used. But, having a lot of money doesn't make you truly wealthy.

There are five forms of wealth; money, time, satisfaction, relationships and health. It is only by having a relative abundance and balance between of all of those that makes you truly WEALTHY.

Each chapter in Living a Wealthy Life is a stand-alone story of gaining an abundance in one or more of the five forms of wealth. They are contributed by people from around the globe. (see their bios at the end) And, at the risk of sounding like a famous movie character, this book is like a box of chocolates. Each story has its own unique flavor and texture.

We believe they will inspire and entertain you. Some stories will make you laugh. Some will make you cry. Others may even make you angry. But, the overall result will be a new perspective on what being wealthy is really all about. We hope in reading this book you will find encouragement, hope and a renewed sense of what's possible for you.

Bob Sager

The Better Dad

Matt Orlando

I have wanted to be a dad for as long as I can remember. Early childhood experiences shaped my thinking and desire to find the love I was missing.

My parents divorced when I was four years old. I can remember two things from my parents' brief marriage. The first was my father bringing home an Atari. The second was the last day my father lived with us. I can remember it like it was yesterday. My parents were in their bedroom closet fighting, my dad was packing his bags, and I was covering my infant brother's ears so he wouldn't hear the fighting going on less than eight feet from where he was lying.

Life changed rather quickly after that fateful day. I went from seeing my father every day, to seeing him sporadically. My aunt, uncles, and grandmother did an excellent job of keeping me connected to my father's side of the family. They were constantly picking me up to spend time with them, regardless of whether my father was there. Unfortunately, there are five or so years where I can't remember spending any time with my dad, at least nothing of consequence. Someone might say I was too young to remember, but I can recall doing dozens of things with other members of my dad's side of the family.

Things weren't much better in my mom's house right after the divorce. Thankfully, we lived in a two-family house with my grandparents who could be role models for me. Although I constantly had arguments with my mother in which she would promptly tell me how much I was like my dad, the fact my grandparents were on the next floor seemed to keep things in check for quite some time. All that changed when I was nine;

my mother remarried, and she moved our family down to South Jersey.

I will never understand why my mother stayed with my step-father. At the time, he was a raging alcoholic who didn't come home after work, crashed cars, and did other stupid things. He wasn't a role model for me and my brother. I spent more time than I'd like to admit sitting in the backseat of my mother's car at 3:00 am while she drove around Atlantic City looking for him.

I spent most of my childhood feeling unloved, and was angry at everyone for the situation I was in. Every relationship I had seemed to be broken in some way. I went from being an outgoing person to an introvert who was afraid to introduce people to my family. I was hiding the dysfunctionality. To this day I wish that my mother had never married my step-father. At the very least, I wish I would have said something to my dad's side of the family instead of keeping them completely in the dark.

I stopped seeing my dad at all by the time I turned fourteen. He had remarried, had more kids, and I felt like I had taken a backseat. I still had a burning desire to feel loved. I wasn't getting it at home and it wasn't coming from the relationship with my dad. The next time I saw him was fifteen years later. I went to my great grandmother's funeral and introduced him to my wife and child.

Feeling beaten and wanting more, I left my mom's house at the age of seventeen. My grandfather had seen an advertisement for a new military school opening. The interview process was tough, but I was determined. I went to four different interviews and eventually was selected to be part of the inaugural class.

Living away from home was great for me. I made a lot of friends and excelled in my new environment. I finished my school work months before everyone else, and was allowed to work on the Air Force base. I was doing data entry while also working at the school helping students find jobs, apply for college, or enter the military after they graduated from high school. I was even lucky enough to start college while everyone else was still taking high school courses. My experience in military school brought a basic level of functionality to my life but didn't really help me with my interpersonal skills, especially when it came to relationships with people I loved.

I've always wanted to feel loved. Who doesn't? It wasn't until the year 2000 that I finally had a chance to start a family and do things the right way.

I met my ex-wife in a Yahoo chat room in October of 2000. It wasn't until Easter Eve in 2001 when we finally met and went on our first date. We immediately hit it off and within a few months of dating were married and expecting our first child.

The birth of our daughter was the most important thing to ever happen to me. I finally felt I had the unconditional love I was longing for. I wanted to be the best father I could possibly be for her. Unfortunately, while my relationship with my daughter was perfect, my marriage was beginning to falter. I'd like to say it wasn't my fault, but the reality was that I had terrible relationship skills. I had learned from the worst.

My ex and I divorced in 2005. On the day of our divorce my ex told me I was a great father but wasn't a great husband. It took me years to come to grips with that statement, and a few more years to finally get to a point where I dealt with the issues I had since my childhood.

After our divorce, my ex moved to Pennsylvania with our daughter to be closer to her family. I resented the move because I wanted to see more of my daughter, not less. I didn't want her to wind up having the same kind of relationship with me that I had experienced with my dad. Ultimately, I decided that it was up to me to continue to be the best Dad I possibly could, and foster a loving, close relationship with my daughter.

My divorce created a few issues that were getting in the way of a great relationship with my daughter:

1. My daughter lived three hours away.

2. I only got to see her every other weekend, and four weeks during the summer.

3. I was working long hours, and I was having a hard time picking her up on Fridays.

4. Spending time with her during the summer was tough, due to my working hours.

There were two things that made me change my thinking and behavior to ensure my daughter and I could spend time together. The first was my four-year-old daughter questioning why she only got to be with me 70 days a year, but she was with her mom for almost 300.

The second experience that finally made me decide to make a change in my life was a court appearance. Because of my job, I was requesting to have the pickup time changed to 7:30 pm from 7:00. I was working in New York City at the time, and getting to the spot to meet my daughter on time was impossible. The judge overseeing the request thought I should just pick my daughter up the next day instead. I cried on the spot. I had her for only 70 overnights a year, and now they wanted to push it down to 52. Thankfully, I was able to get everyone to agree on 7:30 pm. I knew at that moment that I needed to make an almost immediate change in my life for the sake of my relationship with my daughter.

Within a few months of making that decision, I left my position at the email marketing company where I was working and went out on my own.

The first couple of years were extremely tough. I was poor, and whatever money I had went to my daughter. I saved every dollar I could for the summer so I could take her away on vacations during the four weeks I had her. We spent time camping, hiking, going to Disney, and doing other things together. These are traditions my daughter and I continue today because it allows us to spend time together and focus on our relationship.

Ask my daughter today, and she will tell you I'm the greatest dad in the world because I spend all my time with her, teach her things, take her places, and I will travel six hours just to watch her spend five minutes doing a skit at school.

I look at it another way. My daughter is my hero. She travels six hours every other weekend to see me when she could be spending time with her friends. She has taught me how to be a man, a Dad, and most importantly how to love. I wouldn't trade it for all the money in the world.

* * * * *

When Purses Fly

Marlow & Chris Felton

Have you ever felt stuck and frustrated with your financial situation? Have you taken it out on your spouse? We are Chris and Marlow Felton, and we know those feelings well. Ten years ago, when we were first married, we may have appeared to have it all together, but we did not.

Chris:

We both sarcastically refer to when we first got married as," the good old days". Those days were filled with frustration, financial stress, blame, and a lot of hard work without the results to show for it.

Marlow:

I remember when I first met Chris. I thought he was cute and funny. I also thought that, since he used to be a CPA and was in the financial services industry, certainly he was making great financial decisions. I was soon to find out how wrong I was.

Chris:

I remember struggling to keep up with the bills and at the same time not wanting to burden Marlow with the stressful details. I thought for some reason it would be better that way. One day, Marlow came to me asking to help with the bills and to go over a budget. At the time, I thought the word budget was a four-letter word. It was after much contemplation that I had the inspiration that I should let her do it.

Marlow:

Chris was hit with an "aha" moment while meditating. The funny part is he had to meditate in in his car in the garage because our house was so small. He would actually put a winter coat on and go sit in his car to meditate.

But working on a budget was how I found out what was REALLY going on! What I found was a ton of debt, high overhead, and no accountability from Chris. This made me feel very uncertain and scared about our financial future. I also grew more and more frustrated, with most of the frustration focused directly on Chris. But I kept it bottled up inside.

Chris:

I continued to think if we could just make more money, our problems would be solved. We just kept working harder and harder thinking that would magically fix everything. Then one day, I had a large expense to pay for and no money to pay it. We hadn't merged our finances yet and I knew Marlow had some money saved. I didn't want to, but I HAD to ask her for some money. Well I did, and how do you think that went?

Marlow:

To say I lost my temper would be an understatement! I was MAD! I started yelling and screaming at Chris; rattling off all the things I was sick and tired of. It was a long list and the items kept coming. My bottle of frustration just exploded. I felt I needed to make my frustration clearer to him, so I picked up my purse and threw it at Chris. That wasn't clear enough. So, I went over, picked it up and threw it at him again. Blinded by rage, I may not have stopped if Chris hadn't come up with a powerful question...

Chris:

I asked her, "Then why are you married to me?"

Marlow:

That question stopped me in my tracks. That's a great question, I thought. I was so caught up being frustrated and angry that the reasons I had married him had been pushed aside. So now I had to come up with a new list. The "Why I Married Chris Felton List". I decided Chris had some great qualities that I was unwilling to live without. If I was going to stay married to him some things would need to change, but only by shifting my focus to the new list.

Chris:

I knew I needed to change my spending habits for things to work. I was also going to have to let go of my delusion that things would just fix themselves; that I could continue to work harder doing the same things and the money would just come. We both had to get clear on our combined vision for our future in order to move forward together.

Marlow:

What I realized that night was that I had to take responsibility for my actions as well. If Chris was such an idiot, then I was a bigger idiot for marrying him! He wasn't an idiot, but it was still my decision and my choice. We each had to come to grips with our own role in our current reality, accept where we were, let it go, and then design and plan for our ideal life together.

Chris:

Marlow and I refer to this night as the night that changed everything, because it was. We realized we needed to come together as a team toward a dream life. OUR dream life. We started by creating our vision for the future, then decided on the number one thing that would make the biggest difference in our life. We both agreed that having more money saved would make us both feel more secure. That became our focus.

Marlow:

With savings now our number one goal, we put together a financial segregation plan, allocated funds for different purposes and created a budget we could stick to. Most importantly, we determined the weekly amount of money we needed to save to meet our annual goal. Not the annual amount of money but the weekly amount we needed to save. This created a smaller number that seemed more attainable and kept us on track.

Chris:

We tracked every dollar that we were able to save each and every week and celebrated any and all money that came into our life. Celebrating wins, even small, helps to shift your focus to possibilities and away from what is sucking you down! Many people overlook small wins, thinking they aren't significant, when they are! Any step in the right direction is a step in the right direction and should not be overlooked. It should be held as just as important as a leap, and a tool to build momentum. Big wins usually come from small incremental steps toward a goal. We knew every dollar was one step closer to our goals and dreams.

Marlow:

We both look back on those days as the days we laid our financial freedom foundation. We gained a new respect for money and realized what was important. The other things were just taking us further away from our goals and dreams. The significant spending cuts we took back then were a small price to pay to get things moving in the right direction. Getting our mentality about money in the right place was critical, too. While we could penny-pinch our way to financial freedom; we knew we also needed to dramatically increase our income. An interesting thing happened. The more money we saved, the more money we earned. We felt an increased peace of mind with each amount of forward progress. This confidence and clarity opened us to more opportunities to increase our income.

I want to stress the importance of earning more money and working together. Without dramatically increasing our income, we would not have been able to turn our financial situation around. We discussed as a couple on a weekly basis any and all ideas we had to increase our income that week. No matter how small, we had to pursue the most efficient path to increasing our income. Two heads are better than one, especially when they have a vested interest in the success of the "team." Chris and I came up with ideas we may not have come up with individually. We could also talk through how we could implement it together or support each other in making it happen.

Chris:

Since this time 10 years ago, we have significantly turned our financial situation around. We have more than tripled our income, and have grown our net worth exponentially. We learned that wealth is an internal game, not external. The feeling of financial freedom is priceless and worth the years of focus and accountability to each other. We grew more connected as a couple working toward a common goal. We now experience financial freedom and teach others how to do the same.

Marlow:

Our perception of money is forever changed because of this experience. We have respect and clarity in how to use it from an emotional perspective. We can keep ourselves in check when making financial decisions because we know what runs us and the bad programing we have overcome still pops up from time to time. The mental clarity that enables us to make better financial decisions is priceless. It is also easier than it may seem. When you stay focused on your ideal life together and take it one step at a time anyone can get there!

Never Good Enough

Colby Richards

If you had told the 20-year-old me that by the time I was 30, I would experience divorce, unemployment, and bankruptcy - that I would spend most of my 20's and 30's emotionally and spiritually lost, leaving a trail of destruction behind me - I would have replied without doubt or hesitation that you had the wrong guy. History now shows, 20-year-old me would have been very, very wrong.

Isn't it interesting how a person, who was by most measures pretty humble, could be so deceived into believing they had it all figured out? I certainly was. A friend once told me that behind every arrogance hides a level of insecurity. I most certainly was insecure. I was insecure because I was afraid. This fear developed into a level of pride. I was too proud to let anyone know what was really going on inside my head. This created a toxic mix: I was afraid, insecure, and too proud to ask for help. The Proverbs caution, "Pride comes before a fall." And fall, I did. This toxic mix of fear and pride kept me from getting marital help, and my marriage crumbled, one poor choice at a time. It kept me from getting financial guidance, and later had me walking into bankruptcy court. I thought I could do it all alone and ended up devastatingly alone.

To better understand how this all unraveled, it's important to rewind my story a bit. I grew up in a typical blue-collar middle-class family. My parents were committed to one another in their marriage and I had a little sister I adored. We did not live the life of luxury, but we certainly had more than the basics. We always had a roof over our heads, food on the table, and for a period of time - an avocado green station wagon with fake wood panel siding. Life was good.

Growing up, I always knew I was loved. However, sometimes simply knowing you are loved isn't enough. Most things, especially academic, came pretty easily to me as a kid. I had numerous successes and I didn't easily give up. However, I didn't really learn how to process my failures as I was growing up. I frequently walked away from a defeat with the feeling that I didn't measure up in some way. My negative thoughts were out of proportion with what had actually happened. I was good, but I was never good enough. I would often relentlessly chastise myself internally for anything less than a complete victory.

Sadly, my childhood didn't involve modern Internet memes to give me life lessons in the form of pithy words placed on a picture. Instead, fear and insecurity began to take root in my subconscious like strong and stealthy weeds. A garden left to weeds yields no good thing and provides cover for varmints. These varmints infested many areas of my life; fears given root in our minds consciously and subconsciously guide what we become, even when it flies in the face of what we know to be true.

In my late thirties, I floundered through the lingering aftermath of choices I made in my twenties. Looking back at my life from the vantage point of regret, I began to take stock of where things went wrong. A friend mentioned the quote to me: *"Insanity is doing the same thing over and over again and expecting different results."*

Well, I certainly didn't believe I was insane, but the truth of the saying resonated deeply. Its truth was painful, actually. It was a moment of clarity in which I realized I had many more bad days ahead unless I took an honest look at the life choices I was making. As I reflected upon my life to that point, I realized there was no singular moment of devastation that caused my life to go horribly wrong. I also want to be crystal clear that I did not, nor do I now, hold anyone other than me responsible for the poor choices I made in my life. However, I was beginning to see a disturbing emerging pattern in my family that went far beyond my experience.

Through conversations and observations, I saw a pattern that extended back at least two generations before me, and it is highly likely to have started long before that. I am not talking about any kind of genetic physical manifestation. No, the generational malady was much more subtle and insidious than that: My grandfather was clearly well trained in the art of being critical, as was my father, as was I. In my experience and observation, the most effective teaching of this curriculum is through subjecting the pupil to frequent criticism.

Even when I was victorious, there consistently seemed to be something that was picked apart - something I should have or could have done better. I told myself it was constructive criticism, but when this type of thinking is the pervasive train of thought we ride on, it becomes a malicious mental cancer that metastasizes into insecurity and fear. I was insecure about my competence and I was afraid of any brave new ventures that might set me up for more criticism if they didn't quite work out. Worst of all, I didn't dare share my struggles with anyone who could have helped me. Pride borne out of a fear of criticism and embarrassment made certain I never did any such thing. Eventually, I found my harshest critic no longer was external. It was me.

My father did the best he could, armed with what he knew from lessons he was taught. In many ways, he did better than his father, and I am grateful. In fact, one of the most sage and valuable lessons I have ever learned was from my father. He repeatedly taught me: When problems arise, stay calm and keep thinking. This mantra has literally saved my life in numerous situations where panic would have robbed me of clear thinking and yielded a disastrous outcome.

Unfortunately, I only applied it in a reactionary way and, even then, I still only looked to myself for the answers. There was no way I wanted people to know what I was facing, and what was at stake; experience taught me that would only lead to yet another cycle of shame and criticism.

Fear overrode my ability to consider that this beautifully simple and practical rationale could be applied even when things were going relatively well. Pride prevented me from being completely transparent and engaging with trusted advisors to hold me accountable and help me stay on track. Fortunately, hitting rock bottom enough times forced me to re-evaluate and see how I could have handled things differently. Being painfully aware that the path you are on is not going to end well can have that effect.

Had I stayed calm and kept thinking, I would have realized that the spending patterns of my twenties were not sustainable. I would have realized that any embarrassment my ex-wife and I experienced, while a trusted advisor went through our finances behind closed doors, would pale in comparison to the public shame of a bankruptcy filing and hearing later. The pain of a budget is less than the pain of a bankruptcy, and the pain of a budget builds financial wisdom and strength.

Had I stayed calm and kept thinking, I would have mustered the courage to get counseling early on with my now ex-wife and let the chips fall where they may, knowing any pain suffered would have been growing pains, not the withering and lingering pain that is divorce. I would not have cared who knew our relationship needed help. I would have realized that though the rumors may have materialized, so would the support network. We could have inspired others to get help before it was too late for them as well.

Most importantly, had I stayed calm and kept thinking, I would have remembered who I was. I would not have become a slave to the well-ingrained fear and insecurity, but would have been able to stand firmly on my principles and faith to guide me through whatever storms came my way. The confidence of knowing who we are empowers us to do that. The absence of such knowledge leaves our lives to drift into waters no clear-thinking person would choose to be in. When storms come, we act not out of confidence and a winning mindset, but out of fear and defeat.

It has been my experience that when we allow fear to hold a position as co-pilot in our lives, things rarely go well. At some point, we all grow tired and weary, leaving fear to take over the controls. A funny thing happens when one allows their fears to direct their paths: we cease to take the best path and instead take paths we believe will help us best avoid shame and pain. Sadly, these paths lead to more pain and shame than the original problem, and this was where I too often took the wrong fork in the road. Fear causes us to act in various states of panic. In truth, through this mentality, I made more poor choices than I care to remember.

Between the luxury of hindsight and the insights from watching my children develop, I have come to realize that there is perhaps something even more important than teaching people how to succeed and win. Fostering an environment of grace allows them to learn how to process their losses and stay in the game instead of getting stuck in a moment; their failures do not need to define them. An environment of grace creates an atmosphere of acceptance that minimizes the fear of failure. Minimizing the fear of failure builds inner confidence and fosters the willingness to seek help when things aren't going quite right...before it's too late.

Fortunately, my story does not end there. Yours doesn't need to either. As Henry Ford is credited with saying; *"Failure is simply the opportunity to begin again more intelligently."*

Not only have I begun again more intelligently, I have begun again more confidently. By no means do I claim to have it all figured out, and I now realize there is no shame in that. Regardless of what I may or may not have figured out, I do know who I am. I do know that taking action to move things in a better direction delivers far better outcomes than holding back in fear of criticism. Fearfully holding back is about as effective as thinking that closing your eyes will somehow keep you dry when it rains. Every life has its rainy days. Confidence helps prepare for weathering the storms. Fear primes us for victimhood.

Now that I am in a different season of life, I strive to apply this thought process throughout my life:

As a man of faith, I seek greater discipline to stay calm and keep thinking so that the emotions and uncertainties in life don't cause me to lose my bearings, and thus my way. This allows me to remember that the opposite of fear is love, and a life focused on loving others has little room for fear. This approach also has an innate way of keeping my life outwardly focused and on track. It forces me to daily acknowledge that not only do I need grace; I need to extend it to others.

As a husband, I desire to stay calm and keep thinking to hear what my wife is really saying. I must see beyond the emotion of the moment, understand her perspective, and truly honor her. I can only gain such clarity when I restrain myself from harsh criticisms and foster an environment in which she feels secure in expressing herself without fear of critical and emotionally charged reactions.

As a father, I strive to stay calm and keep thinking so I don't magnify little problems and overshadow the things that actually are a big deal. Avoiding excessive criticisms and being consistently generous with grace fosters trust; the kind of trust that has my kids coming to me for guidance as they grow older, not social media or the kid down the street.

Sometimes I succeed spectacularly, and sometimes I fail miserably. It can be a struggle to lavish grace generously and withhold criticisms. Old habits die hard. But, the prevailing direction is a direction of positive growth and maturity, because I have experienced the captivity of criticisms and I now know the freedom of grace. With that mindset, I push back against fear, insecurity, and pride. I move forward with grace and the humility to know I need others, and others need me.

No two lives are identical and, while my journey may not be your journey, I believe these principles have universal application:

Never allow yourself to become too proud to ask for help; a fence at the top of a cliff yields far better results than an ambulance at the bottom.

Be a giver of grace. Work to catch people doing things right. Let them know what they've done well. When they stumble, look to find a redeeming quality to praise. It will serve you and others far better than harsh criticisms. Best of all, in their time of darkness, it will give them a moment to build upon.

Be a receiver of grace. Forgive yourself when you make poor choices. Be willing to accept that failure is not often fatal, and your worst injury takes place when you don't forgive yourself and end up getting stuck in what was only a moment in time.

No matter what your story is or where you may be on life's path, stay calm and keep thinking.

Stay calm and keep thinking so you, *"Don't make a permanent decision about a temporary situation."* (T.D. Jakes)

Gratitude Cured My Depression

Isabella Manetti

Before April 2014, my life was moving along wonderfully. I was living in a beachfront apartment on the Gold Coast, Australia. I was spending my time learning how to run an online business, enjoying walks along the beach, swimming, and doing anything my heart desired. Every night the roar of the surf lulled me to a peaceful dream state. I was living what I perceived to be my perfect life.

Suddenly everything crashed around me. My 79-year-old mother had suffered a severe stroke and was not expected to live. She had not been answering the phone when I rang her twice and had not return my calls. This was unusual, so I rang my brother who lived nearby and asked him to check up on her. He found her on the floor in her computer room; we think she had been like that for two days. The doctors told my brother to gather the family around as she would not pull through. I flew down to Adelaide in South Australia to be by her side

Miraculously, she lived, but the journey to her healing was to be long and arduous. It was evident that she would need care for the rest of her life.

My mother begged me not to put her in a home. This was not an option for me anyway, as my mother was not only my mother, but my friend. We shared many wonderful adventures together; travelling around Europe a few times and she stayed with me in Queensland for a few months nearly every year. So without question, I took on the role of caregiver. I left my beautiful apartment to move back down to

Adelaide (a city I had departed years ago due to the fact I was very unhappy with my life there).

I thought I would be able to cope as a caregiver for my mother simply because of my love for her. The truth was, caregiving is a demanding role and I simply did not have the skills to deal with this role. I had no idea how to cope with it. I never had children so I was thrown in the deep end.

My life was no longer about my needs; it was all about my mother's needs. My freedom had been ripped away from me, and over the next six months I suffered from two emotional breakdowns and was catapulted into a deep depression I could not rise above. It affected my emotional, mental and physical health but, somehow, I found the strength to continue on in my life for the sake of my mother.

It did not help that I had returned to living in a city where I had been so unhappy, and I pined away for my beloved sunny and warm Queensland. When I looked into my future all I saw was bleakness. Living in Adelaide for the rest of my life caring for my mother just made me more depressed and my health spiralled down. I was miserable all the time and it showed.

The only support I received from the Government was monetary. No-one asked me how I was coping or advised where I could go for support as a caregiver. I was handling it alone with no training on how to be a caregiver. I just trusted my instincts. At times, I felt overwhelmed and alone, so the moral support from my friends Linda, Gail, Lee and Dale helped me through many difficult times when I just wasn't coping. If it wasn't for them, I don't know if I could have maintained this life.

By December 2014, I was desperate to feel supported and connected locally as I felt so alone with my demanding responsibilities as a caregiver. I was living in a place that I had never wanted to return to. With my negative attitude towards living in Adelaide and dealing with depression, well, there wasn't much chance I was going to attract any kind of support. My vibration was pretty low.

My girlfriend, Gail, who was my mother's Tai Chi teacher, saw how I was deteriorating emotionally, physically, and mentally, and understood my depression. She advised me to go and see a psychologist. I chose to see one affiliated with the Carers Association but unfortunately, she was of no help whatsoever. What to do next?

Then one wondrous day soon after, the Universe heard my cry for help. I was outside reading my favourite magazine *Living Now*, when an article immediately caught my attention: "Gratitude – A Cure for Depression?"

The author, Toni Powell, had written something which made me realise that because I was replaying the same negative thoughts over and over again, I had created a strong neural pathway which became automated in my brain. She said that it is the strongest neural pathway that becomes our default thinking.

Ms. Powell suggested to deliberately think grateful, thankful, good thoughts in order for one's brain to begin thinking positively. By simply deciding each day to look for the good in my life and express gratitude meant that my brain would become alert to good, positive things instead of the bad, negative things I was focusing on.

I had read years ago, about the importance of keeping a "gratitude journal", but I decided instead to create a Facebook Group and a personal blog on gratitude. I chose this strategy because I wanted the Universe to know that I was really serious about finding things to be grateful for, even though I thought I had no reason for gratitude. It was worth a try. I wanted to declare it to the whole world. I decided to expect good things to happen to me and that more would come back to me to be grateful for.

So, every day without fail I posted the things I was grateful for in my Facebook Group and blog. Nothing elaborate. Just things like; a sunny day; watching a great TV show; enjoying learning and working on my online business; friends who cared about me; delicious meals; comfortable bed; heating; air-conditioning; domestic cleaner; the progress my mother was making, etc.

Within a few weeks, good things did start happening in my life. Lee, a girlfriend of mine in Adelaide who I have known for 40 years, rang to invite us to visit. If my mother and I were interested in staying with them any time after Christmas Day they had a vacant granny flat for my mother and a room for me. "Absolutely" I said. My spirits lifted immediately!

Lee and her husband live in one of the most idyllic areas of the city; the Adelaide Hills. I have always had an affinity for "The Hills", as this is where I was born. At five years of age I moved with my family into a suburban area where I grew up, and was very unhappy. My mother and I visited with Lee and her husband for six lovely days. The tiredness caused by her stroke meant my mother was usually in bed by 7:00 pm, but on New Year's Eve she stayed up after midnight and even enjoyed a few glasses of champagne. We intended to stay longer (I wasn't in a hurry to return), but due to an imminent raging bush fire we were warned to evacuate the area. However, in those six days I felt such a sense of relief as they cared for my mother whenever I needed to rest. The sole responsibility for caring for her was lessened by each of us caring for her. I felt so rejuvenated and blessed, so I was very grateful to them.

Lee drove my mother and myself for a tour around "The Hills' and as passengers we enjoyed ourselves immensely.

Upon returning to my mother's home she seemed sad. To my delight, the next day she announced she no longer wanted to live in her home and desired to move to the Gold Coast with me. I gave her the biggest thankful hug. Both of us were so happy about this decision. It was especially momentous for my mother, as she was leaving her home of 52 years.

At long last my depression lifted remarkably.

We sold my mother's home and purchased a unit in a retirement village on the Gold Coast sight unseen via the internet. One of my mother's friends had told her how great it was living in an independent living centre in Adelaide. Unfortunately for my mother, living on her own was now impossible after her stroke. But it gave me the idea to check out independent living centres on the Gold Coast. Time after time, the same company kept coming up in all my searches. Out of their four centres, the one I liked the most had a few units for sale and one of them was affordable for us. Two of my girlfriends, one living on the Gold Coast and the other in Brisbane, offered to check out this centre on my behalf. As it turned out, it was not suitable for my mother because it was very hilly, the garage was a distance away from the unit and the unit had a step inside. They recommended the Southport centre. Southport had only one unit left, so in faith I bought it, believing it would be perfect. I had no doubts whatsoever. I trusted in the Universe that I had purchased the right home.

I will never forget the moment we arrived. We drove into the centre and we both fell in love with it. It was perfect, especially for my mother as every amenity was in walking distance with her walker. When we moved into our new home my girlfriend Dale, who lives an hour away, helped us with organising curtains.

I am so blessed with caring girlfriends and with the many wonderful new friends I have made in the village who assist me whenever I need a hand to care for my mother. My mother also loves living here, has made friends and her health has improved greatly.

I realise how hard it is to stop feeling sorry for yourself and to stop focusing on the bad things in your life. However, all of us have the ability and the opportunity to cultivate an "attitude of gratitude" because it is free.

Instead of complaining about all the things that are wrong in your life, take a few moments to focus on all that you have, the beauty in the everyday, expressing gratitude to others; becoming more mindful, enjoying the sound of the wind, the chirping birds, the butterflies, the bees, a delicious meal, friends, family, loved ones, an act of kindness from a stranger etc.

There is much research which supports the idea that practicing gratitude on a daily basis rewires our brains for the better—it is a truly powerful life-changing tool. So, if your life is not working for you right now, I would suggest practising daily "an attitude of gratitude."

Complete Me

Malavika Vivek

Dissatisfaction has a myriad of forms. Much of the time, it seeps in – you don't even know it's there. At least that's how it was for me. It dragged me down and I didn't even realize what I was feeling. I think that the routine of daily life masks it a lot; it was a question that someone asked me that caused me to examine myself closer. And when you do that, when you see that you aren't as happy as you could be or should be, it can be hard to feel anything but lost. This is why I'm a firm believer in leaning in and listening to other people's stories – this is how you help yourself. Welcome to my story.

I entered high school feeling like I could do anything. I felt as if the world was mine to conquer and my mind was filled with a million different plans and goals. Making plans and goals is great, but it can often lead you in the direction of what I'm going to call false satisfaction. They made me feel complete somehow, as if making them meant I was going to achieve everything I dreamed of. But I was missing the most crucial part of all of this. You need a motive to achieve anything and, especially when your goals are as big as mine were, you need an unfaltering drive and belief in what you are doing. I, like many of my classmates, had my sights set on the most elite colleges in the country.

I grew up in Edison, New Jersey, and living in a town like Edison, you are practically raised hearing about extraordinary students and their perfect SAT scores and perfect extracurriculars. Edison is unique because of its huge Indian population – my parents and many of my friends' parents were immigrants from different parts of India. The struggle they had to go through to create a better life for their families in America caused them to place an extreme emphasis on academics for their children. From elementary school, my friends' parents only spoke of the "perfect" students who achieved straight As and got accepted to Ivy League schools. Though I was fortunate enough to have parents who didn't put any pressure on me, I grew up hearing about these students described in the highest regard and this became my ideal.

Through elementary and middle school, I aimed for perfection – excellent grades, participation in too many clubs, advanced honors coursework. I often heard of this "recipe" for college admissions – play a sport, get amazing grades and test scores, start a club or have some leadership role, and have some artistic talent. Apparently, having each of these components would show an Ivy League admissions committee that you were a well-rounded student deserving of entering their hallowed halls. I grew so enamored with this idea and even when I achieved these perfect grades, I still didn't feel complete.

I remember a time in fifth grade towards the end of the year, when I had this streak of perfect scores on math tests. My teacher, seeing how bored I was, challenged me to keep it up and I did, receiving only perfect scores on math tests. However, I was still not happy and this confused me. I had gotten everything I wanted – so why wasn't I happy? I ignored that feeling then, telling myself that everything would be fine as I started with a clean slate in middle school. After all, I had no reason to not be happy; I was working hard to go to the best of colleges. This is where I took my second step toward dissatisfaction. When you simply conform to an ideal without understanding why you want to be a certain way, you can wake up one day and just not know the point of anything you are doing.

Middle school and my first year of high school were more of the same. I did taekwondo and while I began it because I was genuinely interested in the martial art, I was driven to continue by the many people who commented that it would look great on a college application. I also began singing in my school's choir and while again, I joined this because it was a good extracurricular, I truly fell in love with being part of a choir. It was like being part of a team and my friends in choir weren't all honors students or workaholics; we were just people who all loved to sing. I began to relax more in singing, especially when I wasn't stressed about getting into the honor choirs that would look good on applications. Music became somewhat of a refuge for me as I kept pushing away the feelings that told me something was missing from my life.

While I continued choir in high school, I had to pursue it through private classes because of the workload from the high school I chose to attend. Due to my interest in engineering and technology, I decided to take the admissions test to attend my county's vocational school which specialized in science, technology, engineering and mathematics (STEM). As a student at 'the Academy' (the abbreviated name students fondly called it), my schedule consisted of eighty-eight minutes of engineering every day in addition to the regular high school coursework. The Academy is also a small high school with only about 40 talented students per grade, and as a newly accepted student I soon found out that this fosters a competitive, albeit collaborative, environment. There was a strong sense of family among the students across the grade levels; we were all in this struggle together. The struggle that brought us all closer? College applications, of course.

As a feeder school to some of the top universities in the country, college applications and the merits and drawbacks of every college are often discussed, argued about, analyzed, and dissected at the Academy. Colleges were discussed like players on fantasy football teams; MIT v. Stanford, Harvard v. Princeton. The students spoken about in the highest regard were the few that led many of the schools' clubs. Naturally, I joined most of these clubs; everything from Model United Nations to Debate, Math League to Future Business Leaders of America. By the end of freshman year, I quit most of the clubs save for a few that had actually become meaningful to me. While this was a step in the direction of being happy, I went into that summer feeling like I hadn't accomplished enough. I still felt like I was moving without reason.

During sophomore year of high school, someone asked me why I worked so hard. And I realized that was the first time I had ever been forced to take a hard look at what I was doing. What was the point? To get into a good college? What was the point of that? I knew I could find work after high school with my skillset in tech and knowledge of business. Having a father who started a software company and literally living in the startup environment since I was nine, I learned a lot about what it took to get hired. I observed a business being built firsthand and listened in on conference calls day and night. So even though it was a lot easier for me to believe that college was necessary to get a good job, I knew better. I honestly did not know why I wanted to go to college.

I read articles on James Altucher's blog on the numerous reasons why college is simply a waste of time and money – I hadn't even considered this perspective. I agreed with him that I had been "brainwashed" by society to think that going to college is the only way to have a stable, successful life. As someone who intended to major in computer science, a cursory glance at the courses I would take over four years immediately told me that much of what I would learn would be of little to no use in the real world. This was when I truly realized I did not know what I wanted. This path that had seemed crystal clear was now just lost in a fog. Our feelings of satisfaction are most often tied to our feelings of purpose and direction, and I had just lost any semblance of purpose I had.

Feeling directionless can be one of the loneliest feelings in the world. I think it's because it is a more complex feeling than happiness or sadness; it is multi-dimensional so it's hard for people around you to empathize. To most of the outside world, it seemed I was one of the most driven people they knew but I was learning that drive is useless without knowing what direction to drive in. This is when I learned perhaps the most important lessons when it comes to satisfaction – feeling satisfied is all about feeling passionate about something. Satisfaction is something you can give yourself by believing in not only what you do but why you do it. And, as I forced myself to ask the hard questions about what it is I wanted to do with my life, I found my passion.

Prior to this period of self-scrutiny, I had found myself reading more and more scientific articles from various journals published on the web. It was when I was doing a biology assignment that I happened to come across an article about epigenetics and its applications in food allergy. As someone with an extremely allergic family member and a developing interest in genetics, I was keen to learn more. As I looked closer into the field, I realized that my knowledge of computer science could be applied to analyze the large sets of data involved in the study of epigenetics and food allergy. I delved deeper into machine learning techniques and other methods of data analysis that could help make sense of this data. I reached out to many researchers and pored through numerous online resources – every answer I found just seemed to lead to more questions.

Finally, the cold-emailing led me to a great mentor at the Children's Hospital of Philadelphia. He allowed my partner and I to observe and helped us understand many of the datasets. In the end, this helped us create a machine learning algorithm to improve diagnostics in allergy. And while this may seem wholly unrelated to my personal satisfaction journey, it is a very crucial part of it. This research represented a period of accelerated learning in my life and it made me feel excited about my life again. Every day I woke up with a mission and went to sleep dreaming about finding solutions. This also made me realize that I wanted to go to college as long as I was learning something; this was when I discovered cognitive science. Cognitive science was the field that combined my interests in machine learning, biology, and artificial intelligence. The ironic thing? I had found my passion and as a result, satisfaction, just when I had stopped looking for it.

Another very special thing happened around the same time as I was getting into research. As a woman in STEM and moreover, a woman of color, it had always been a part of my mission to advocate for more women in STEM. My struggle had always been parlaying that mission into an organization or into some way of affecting real change. In sophomore year, I began the Women Tech eXchange, a speaker series in my school that features female leaders in tech and business. This was inspired by the National Center for Women and Information Technology, a community of women across the nation that shared the same passion I had for technology. This community showed me that there were so many positive female role models in tech fields who could inspire many more young women. This was the next step to building satisfaction – helping others like me and watching these young women light up with the possibility of new ideas and opportunities drove me to overcome all the obstacles I ran into with my organization.

The ultimate piece of my journey towards building satisfaction came to me at the Watermark Conference for Women I attended recently. As I spoke to some female entrepreneurs in a think tank for young women, there was one piece of advice that seemed almost universal – say yes. Say yes even when you don't know how, or if you aren't sure you are ready, or you are scared you aren't good enough. That sentiment made me feel so empowered. When another high schooler asked my women in tech community if anyone would be interested in co-leading a workshop for middle school girls with her, I saw an opportunity to impact even more direct change. This workshop transformed me; armed with the strength to create our own opportunities, we taught 40 middle school girls how to build apps and create social impact with them. Soon enough, our workshop turned into Girls Make Apps, a national organization, and we were creating similar initiatives to introduce even more women into the field. This kind of impact, this kind of giving, taught me that we all draw satisfaction from inspiration as well.

Expecting our satisfaction to not change is unrealistic. As we grow as people and our priorities become different, our satisfaction will be based on different things. As far as I've seen with the many different people I have met in my journey as a woman in tech, researcher, and high school student, passion drives satisfaction. The funny thing about passion is you can't force it – it must come from within. I stumbled onto what I was passionate about by just finding something I was really interested in and becoming curious about it. The other important lesson I've learned is that while goals can be a great way to maximize potential, they can also lead to false satisfaction and it is important (albeit difficult) to recognize this. And finally, while satisfaction may seem like an isolated journey, it is the act of helping people and empowering others that will really make a difference in your life. When you inspire, you become inspired and in the end, it is this feeling that makes us complete.

* * * * *

What If...?

Spike Humer

It took forever to get there but it happened overnight.

I woke up in the middle of the night with a pounding heart, a racing mind, and a conflicted soul.

"What if..."

My mind was being flooded with waves of uncertainty. My thoughts were being tossed from side-to-side and crashing against the rational barriers of my brain. I felt on the verge of panic, and I'm not a panicking kind of guy. I didn't know what do or what to say. I didn't even know who, what, or how to ask.

The mental tsunami started to subside. But the landscape of my brain still was littered with the debris of my shattered and scattered thoughts.

I was filled with uncertainty and a need to understand something I couldn't comprehend. I didn't even know the questions, and I sure as hell didn't know the answers. I just knew something wasn't right and something had changed. My mind was racked with fear and insecurity.

Maybe it was just the signs of an aging body and a "maturing" mind. Whatever the cause, I began to understand the condition. I wasn't happy and for the first time in a long time, I was afraid.

It wasn't that I was just unhappy in a bluesy kind of way. I felt empty on the inside and drained from the outside. The kind of empty a banana peel must feel when it's stripped from its fruit and put on the compost pile. Purposeless... as if the juice and the joy had been bled from my mind and my heart. It wasn't overly painful, just unfamiliar and more than a bit disorienting.

The things I placed the most meaning in seemed unimportant. Work was routine—routinely stressful, routinely uncertain, and routinely shaky. I was burning all the candles from both ends and losing money in the middle—lots of money! I had gone through a series of bad deals, busted business ventures, and broken dreams. Most of my work days for almost two-years were split between equal shifts of anxiety and depression, with a dash or two of anger, and heaps of frustration.

I was consumed by doubt and obsessed with simple survival. My days were predicable. Getting out of bed was a chore. Staying in bed was worse. I'd drag myself up with a small dose of hope and optimism, and be slapped silly by noon with the reality of where I was and what I had created in my business and career.

Work-free weekends were a myth. Holidays were dragons meant to be slayed by the hour so I could get back to the business of trying to get my income train back on track. Birthdays, anniversaries, and gatherings with friends weren't points of celebration as much as they were inconveniences and monuments of my frustration because I "needed" to work.

In life, in business, and in my relationships, I was going through the motions and the motions had lost their meaning. Looking back, the only real anchor I felt was my marriage and my wife's support. Not that I didn't have friends and other family members who cared, I just never shared my thoughts, feelings, fears, or frustrations. I started to withdraw: disconnecting socially, professionally, and emotionally. I was swimming and beginning to drown in debt, desperation, and isolation. Even time with my wife started to dwindle in frequency and diminish in quality.

Something had to change and fast!

Torn between wanting to know why and how I got to where I was, and feeling sorry for myself, I found spaces of light and insight, sometimes small and dim but hope-instilling.

The months leading up to the near collapse had been building for years. I ignored the signals and closed my eyes to the signs. Several friends told me I was taking too many risks, some politely, some more directly. I heard their voices but was deaf to their advice. I just kept working—harder and longer and dumber. I jumped into one start-up after another—big upside businesses that had lots of potential, but were fraught with uncertainty and instability. I lost my zest and my zeal; and I started to let deadlines pass out of mental, physical, and emotional paralysis.

When the first deal died, I doubled down on the next. I went from a small start-up venture that had little capital, to an enterprise that had little more than a vision with fragments of a structure. "Swing harder, work longer," became my mode of operation and my emotional mantra. I invested my time, money, talent, and connection currency to try and put some meat on the bones of a skeleton start-up.

Strike Two.

I had some mini-successes along the way, mainly in coaching and consulting with small stable businesses. A few clients here and there. A one-off deal or two kept the bills paid, but not enough to slow the spiral. Seeing some successes with my coaching and consulting clients helped keep me slightly in the circle of sanity, but I was bumping the edge. My unhappiness was turning into a blanket of panic and anxiety I couldn't throw off. Helping others wasn't enough to offset the fear of drowning in a sea of debt and decline. I began to doubt my own ability to help others, since I wasn't able to help myself. If felt incongruent and inauthentic, which only exacerbated my state of internal and external affairs. I thought, "Maybe I just don't have it anymore." What's worse, I began to wonder if I ever had it to begin with.

Every imaginable form of wealth in my life was being drained. I was spending more time making less money, at the expense of my health, relationships, and quality of life. My back was against the wall and the wall wasn't moving. Something had to give.

My wife Michele is the sweetest, gentlest person I have ever known. She gave me more than the nudge I needed. After weeks on end of being shaken awake night after night with the recurring 'What if?' question, we spent a pivotal day together. Me mainly in detached silence, and Michele trying to pry and pull conversation and connection out of me. That evening my wife said. "You've always been the strongest person I know…" She didn't need to add the word "but…" or add the exact examples of what had changed in me and in our life. I knew the evidence was there but Michele was being too kind to call me out directly. Those eight words spoke to me in volume and in volumes.

For years, I've told others that there is a certain kind of strength in reaching out and asking for help. Easy to say, hard to do for most. For me it's always been just short of impossible.

I like to think of myself as humble, but I am a proud man. Being a "fixer" for others most of my life, asking for help was never in my vocabulary. Life and my wife had given me no choice.

Finally, I reached out.

Some of the great blessings I have in my life are the people I've met and the people I know. I have friends, colleagues, and clients around the world. People with incredible experience, insights, success and wisdom in virtually every area of life and business.

Out of the thousands of contacts and the dozens of friends I have, there are but a handful that I trust with my life. The kind of friends that are family and who I refer to as "movers in the middle of the night". You know the type; the friends you could call in the middle of a dead-sleep, and they'd answer. If you asked them to come to your house right away and help you move, they'd be there in an instant. The kind of friends who, when you have two, you'd gladly give them one; if you had one you'd give them half no questions asked.

I made the calls—four to be exact. The meetings were set. My buddy Mel met me in Vegas. Darren flew over from Australia. Bruno and I met in San Diego. Brian brought me to his house in Tahoe. I laid out the situations with unvarnished truth. No sugarcoated, candied-up conversations. No blame. No shame. No "shoulda-woulda-coulda" kind of crap. Just plain talk about where I was and what I needed to change.

We worked through the obstacles, we explored the opportunities. We put plans in place. We set up check-ins and checkups for accountability. We pared down the process to a handful of actions; what to do, and what not to do, what to do more of, and what to do less of.

The first order of business was bringing back some balance in my life. Simple things at first like getting back to the gym.

Making an effort to reconnect socially, spiritually, and emotionally. Making time for the people I love, and spending time writing, reflecting, reading, and thinking. None of these actions or activities are overly complex or difficult to do. But when you're in a race of desperation they are often the first things to dwindle or die.

Next, implementing the criteria of what to keep, what to give up, and what to pursue or leave alone in business. It meant "firing" some clients, "quitting" some projects, and surrendering the possibility of the next homerun at the expense of just getting back in the game. I created exact criteria of what I was looking for in business opportunities. I shortened my operating horizons on return-on-effort and lowered my risk-threshold. I minimized my tolerance for uncertainty and only pursued opportunities that fit the brand-new criteria. I decided anything I was going to apply my time, talent, and energy to had to meet a different set of standards. First, it had to have pretty high probability of success. I only wanted, and was willing to pursue, opportunities that fit my new trifurcated mantra of "I only want to work on things where I could do some good, have some fun, and make some money."

I left behind potentially lucrative deals that might not work, deals that might have only marginal impact, and deals that meant working on things that didn't matter to me or with people I could only tolerate. It seemed like it took forever but it happened virtually overnight. The extrinsic results weren't immediate but the intrinsic rewards happened almost instantly.

My passion started to rekindle. My confidence was beginning to spark and my passion was beginning to burn. Money and material things didn't magically appear overnight, but some of the richness of life became more evident. Weeks and months passed and I began to feel more prosperous and abundant. Some of the lost treasure of traditional wealth began to return.

Remembering that success is a journey and not an event, I began to focus on not just the outcomes I intended, but the processes I was committed to along the way.

I was reminded of the real measures of wealth and the true meanings of life and living. The only treasures to pursue and to possess are: to be healthy, to have someone you love, to spend time doing what you enjoy, and the means and money to learn, grow, and explore. While I'm not "all the way back", I'm truly blessed beyond measure and increasing my five forms of wealth every day.

* * * * *

A Lesson from the Bottom of a Haystack

Beth Perkel

My grandfather saw his life as if he had been born twice: once from his mother's womb and once from underneath a haystack.

During the ravages of World War II, my grandfather found himself fleeing from a band of Nazis on foot. Out of breath, out of options, and even worse, seemingly out of luck, he found himself in a farmer's field. The Nazis were approaching and he quickly buried himself under one of the countless haystacks in sight. Reaching the field and not seeing their desired victim, one of the Nazi's picked up a pitchfork and began stabbing the stacks, suspecting that their target was hidden within one. It was at that moment that my grandfather determined that his time was up, and considered his life as if it was over. He was merely a young adult at the time, had not yet started a family or career or even fallen in love. There were so many adventures yet to be had, so many goals to create and solidify in his young mind let alone reach, and it was all being smothered at the bottom of a haystack as he waited for the sharp tongs to pierce his skin.

If only I had more time, he thought. *Time could solve everything.*

Fast forward several decades. I was born and met my grandfather when he was already an old man. Old not only in years, but severely aged in physical ability. Parkinson's Disease and cancer both slowed him down considerably and he had suffered greatly in his life: Each one of his 10 siblings had been murdered in concentration camps and acts of anti-Semitism in World War II, and after the war the only relative he was able to find and reconnect with was a distant cousin who lived far off across an ocean. Penniless, without virtually any education or knowledge of English, my grandfather made his way to America, the land of opportunity. He had but three treasures that came with him across the ocean: His wife, a new baby, and the gift of time. He had survived. He had prevailed. He had continued onward, and the time he now had was all a miraculous gift.

My grandfather struggled to rebuild a new life in America, but still managed to be extremely happy in the process. He took the time to appreciate the small things in life, and most importantly he never seemed to rush. Whether it was enjoying a sandwich, writing a letter by hand or taking a walk to chat with his many grandchildren, my grandfather did it slowly and with care. He savored time, and time seemed to savor him back.

One summer, while away at camp, I was the recipient of one of my grandfather's hand-written letters. By then his Parkinson's was severe and it was extraordinarily difficult for him to do even the simplest of activities with his hands. My father reported that it took my grandfather the entire day to write it and it showed in each swooping letter, curved every few millimeters by a shaking hand. The surface area of a letter "s" alone was daunting to look at, a jagged construct almost reminiscent of a connect-the-dots done by a small child. The letter arrived in my small, suntanned, preteen hands just as I was feeling particularly vulnerable at camp.

It was my first time away from home for any extended period and I was miserable, homesick and just generally feeling lost and powerless. I was having a terrible summer. We were forced to go on a camping trip where we had to build our own tents out of sheets without any fasteners, or poles, or hardware (let alone instructions as to how), so many of us ended up sleeping without shelter, and woke up soaking wet by the torrential rain that arrived overnight. We went on a similar outdoor excursion that I had no interest in, and my face had so many bug bites in the morning that it significantly altered my appearance. I was bunk mates with a sleepwalker that used to wake me up at night, and sometimes even crawl into my bed so I had no personal space even within my own bunk. The list went on. I had written to my parents several times that I wanted to come home and each letter was met with firm resistance. I was told that this was a good growing opportunity for me and I needed to stay at camp. I remember daydreaming that this whole period of time called 'childhood' could just be fast-forwarded to a time when I'd be able to make my own decisions and not be forced to go places or do things I did not want to. I wanted to grow up as soon as possible and bypass all the actual growing up that that required.

My grandfather's letter reached me just as I was in the throes of self-pity and a desire to fast-forward time. My parents had filled him in on my disdain for camp and his words contained advice on how to appreciate the simple things there, even just peacefully observing the farm animals and nature. Looking at his swooping letters and kind words, and knowing as I did the backdrop of his life, I couldn't help but think how lucky I was to have this time and childhood in general, a luxury he never experienced properly during his younger war-torn years. His letter was one of the most precious possessions I ever received from my grandfather and it reminded me at the right moment a lesson about the wealth of time. Even its very labored creation was wondrous! It showed me that when something is important to someone, it doesn't matter how much time it takes. We rush too much through our lives, but if something is important to us we don't rush it, we give it the time it needs because time is a treasure. The letter sits in an old cigar box from him, preserved with love and resting there for a quarter of a decade to date.

A few years after the letter, on his actual deathbed, my grandfather revealed the story of the haystack for the first time to my father and his sisters.

"Don't be sad for me when I die now," he implored them. "Do not think about the years ahead that I will never live. Think about my time as having ended under that haystack. Every moment after that has been a gift, a treasure. I made a deal with G-d that day decades ago that if he would extend my life even one day I would forever be grateful. And look how many moments, days, and years I got... dying now is something to rejoice over."

It is in this way that he actually saw his death as a tremendous success. He had lived on borrowed time from the Master of the Universe for decades. He had seen his children and grandchildren. He had been granted a new life the minute he heard the pitchfork tossed away in frustration after all the haystacks the Nazis had chosen to stab were found to be empty.

As the Nazis treaded away that day there was silence; only the sounds of renegade strands of hay blowing off to flit about the field, and one racing heart beneath a haystack remained. And it was in that silence, within that first new moment of time that my grandfather had previously considered lost forever, that my grandfather was reborn.

I was 13 years old when my beloved grandfather passed away. The story from his deathbed has clung to me ever since, like remaining bits of hay that can't seem to be shaken off. It taught me the incredible tools of perspective and appreciation of time. I will cherish those lessons forever, along with the note that took him an entire day to write to me and the memory of his aging legs, walking alongside me on a summer's stroll, with nowhere to rush off to and time only to savor.

Wealth Hidden in a Shirt

Craig Fernandes

It was the fall of 2015 and my son, 17-year-old high school Junior Brady Fernandes, was finishing up his shift as a retail clerk at Kinnucan's Outfitters where he had been employed for the last two years. It was as he was putting inventory away, that the idea for creating a line of apparel came to him. He had been thinking about a plan for his Capstone Project; which is a requirement for every graduate from Christian Academy of Knoxville. This Project requires students to find something that interests them which could be a springboard to the next step after high school, and has a philanthropic purpose as well. Some students coached teams for disadvantaged youth, others held bake sales to raise money for charity. Brady decided to use his experience in retail and his eye for style to develop a line of patriotic apparel. His plan was to sell the apparel and use the proceeds to raise money for local non-profit organizations that support wounded veterans. You see, Brady's grandfather was a veteran and he had friends and family members that served in the military. This and the needs of veterans being highlighted in the news and political landscape helped Brady decide to do something that would continue beyond this project.

By definition, a Patriot is a person who vigorously supports their country and is prepared to defend it against enemies or detractors. Threads is often used as a slang word for clothing. So, when you put the two together you get a brand of clothing that shows support for country and for those who fought to defend freedom. Brady's first design was the outline of the United States with a bow tie ribbon strapped across the entire country. When I asked Brady what this original design meant – he said, "The ribbon represents a proper Southern look which appeals to my generation, and more importantly is a throw-back to the days when people would tie a yellow ribbon around their trees to show support for the troops."

From that first classic red white and blue American flag design, Brady moved into state themes and popular local school colors to have a more home town appeal. This reaches people on a local level, allows them to show off their pride for their state and is tail gate worthy as well.

When Brady asked me to help him with his project, I immediately said yes as I saw it as an opportunity to spend time building my relationship with my son. I am a business consultant by trade, which made this a fun challenge for me. One of my roles was to contact the potential non-profits organizations and set up meetings where Brady could show them his Patriot Threads apparel and propose fundraising for them at their events.

It turns out this project was also a lesson in cultivating relationships, the power of networking and gratitude. We needed a local company to print the shirts, and someone at Brady's school recommended a screen printing company called Threds. One of the owners also had children at Brady's school so they understood the project. We needed a mentor in the industry, and Keith Phillips, the other owner of Threds, decided right away that he believed in our cause and would mentor us. We needed a designer to help turn Brady's rough ideas into a finished product, and their designer, Ryan McCray stepped up. The relationships with Keith and Ryan have been a huge part of our ability to launch the brand and keep it going.

So now we had shirts to sell, but still needed a veteran's organization to support; one that was willing to give Brady a chance to sell his shirts at one of their fund-raising events. A google search on Veteran Fund Raisers in Knoxville led us to Project Healing Waters Fly Fishing. They help disabled veterans with their recovery by teaching them how to tie fly's and taking them on guided fly fishing trips into nearby Tennessee streams. Steve Thompson is our main contact there and he let Brady come to their monthly meeting to meet the Veteran volunteers. They were gracious enough to let Brady set up at their next event which was "Pint Night" at River Sports Knoxville. People loved our shirts and we raised an amazing $200 for the organization at that kick-off event. Not bad for a high school project! The biggest impact on us from the event, however, was from the conversations we had with the Veterans who told us their stories and thanked Brady and I for what we were doing for them.

It was at this point that we realized that Patriot Threads could be much bigger than a school project, and become something that Brady could possibly turn into a viable company of its own. I knew that Brady's story was a special one and hoped that some of the local media outlets would consider writing an article or covering our story on the local news. We had seen how the Veterans and the community were supportive of what Brady was doing and thought that if we could reach a broader audience that it would only help us to help more veterans. I reached out to local radio station WOKI and spoke with Bob Yarbrough, a well-respected news-talk radio show host who used to live in my neighborhood. When I told him Brady's story, he loved it and agreed to have us on in February 2016. We are very grateful to him for the opportunity to share our story and mission as guests on the *Howell and Yarbrough Show*.

Two months later, I reached out to the same radio station and Hallerin Hilton Hill agreed to let Brady share his story from a Father and Son angle. This second show added additional validation to our mission and widened the reach within

Knoxville. Brady and I were also able to meet with Knox County Mayor Tim Burchett and Knoxville City Mayor Madeline Rogero, who connected us with the veteran support team they had assembled. Things were moving in the right direction and what followed was another answer to prayer. *The Knoxville News Sentinel* decided to do a front-page story on Patriot Threads as a Father and Son business in the Sunday Father's Day edition in 2016, which included a follow up full page photo and story in the business section of that paper. To this day, it is that article most people mention when I ask how they heard about us. After the newspaper article ran, I reached out to some local television news reporters and they were much more open about doing a story on Brady. What followed was a series of local TV News stories by WATE and WVLT over July 4th weekend and a *Live At 5* appearance of Brady and I along with Matt Zaczyk, our University of TN brand ambassador and apparel model.

We knew that we had something special in our designs and that our cause struck a chord in the hearts of people in the community who wanted to support our veterans. Brady and I decided the next logical step would be to see if the brand could have a following in retail stores as well, so I contacted 3 local game day apparel retailers. We were ecstatic, to say the least, when Brady and I met with buyers for each of these stores and they all agreed to place stocking orders to carry our shirts. We took a risk and attended 2 retail trade shows to expand our reach and customer base. From those shows we received orders from 40 additional retailers in 13 Southern States for our Game Day Line of Patriotic Apparel. At that point, we knew that at least the boutique retailers near southern colleges were willing to give Patriot Threads a shot.

So far, we have raised over $5000 for 15 different local non-profits. Each event has changed us for the better and makes us more committed to our cause. This has been an amazing high school project, but Brady has set his sights much higher for his brand and its mission to raise awareness and support for Veterans and other worthy causes. There are over 22 million veterans in the United States and many of them are disabled or are just forgotten. We want to change that by using Patriot Threads "Apparel with a Purpose" to start a movement across the entire country.

We are blessed to have the support of our community. The small-town atmosphere of Knoxville TN, and the Volunteer State are perfect for our company because we exist to serve others as our primary mission. It is very important to have a purpose that transcends your business. There are plenty of companies out there that make great products, but to separate yourself from the others you really should have at least part of your corporate mission be focused on helping others. Do not be afraid to fail; you will learn so much from the process it will be worth the learning experience.

These experiences have brought us closer together, as it has helped Brady think more about how much I support him and am there for him to help in his success. Brady had never had the opportunity to give a live interview for a newspaper story before, so I had the chance to help him with his confidence. Brady practiced for the interview by telling me his story as if I had never heard it. The reporter came to our house to interview us, which made Brady more comfortable and was also very sweet. He can be confident that I always have his back. Our relationship has grown, as I was there for the interviews to give him support and confidence. We always went out for a celebratory dinner together after the filming. He was the focus of the interviews, but we knew that we were now a family business that would continue to grow, both in sales and in our family bond.

I have also grown through this experience as it has honed my business skills and has also changed the way I view my purpose. The best way to say it is that I was blind and now I see. I used to have goals that were primarily focused on my own personal success – and I have now shifted my motives and core mission to always include helping others as a guiding principle in my future business ventures. When you are exposed to the great need in our society – there is no way you can remain unchanged by it.

Behind the Facade

Mark Brodinsky

Next to gratitude, this might be the most significant guiding principle in life. Yet how do we achieve it, and how do we know when we've arrived?

In my own life, I know the deal now, but it took me years to come to the conclusion. Satisfaction is all based on a few simple needs – the need to be seen, to be valued, to be heard, and the biggest ones; acceptance and love. How many times in life do we pretend we are someone that we are not because we want everyone to like us? Does that leave us feeling satisfied? Maybe for a short time, but not for long. How often do we feel that if we don't succumb to the whims, fancies and expectations of other people – that they won't like us? We live in fear – fear that if we truly revealed ourselves: our unique differences and gifts, who we were born to be, what purpose we have here on this earth - that others will reject us. Yet at the same time it is they too, those who stand in judgment, who are not being their true selves.

It is a satisfaction-less life.

How many of us are really being who we were meant to be, living the life we were meant to live? If we just stepped out from behind the facade with a bold, focused sense of self, that's the life the world would take notice of and even more importantly, would benefit from! For many of us this is scary. I know I was scared; I lacked the courage. But no more.

From the time I was little, I loved to create: to write, to volunteer, and be up on the stage. I remember performing in a play in elementary school, dressed as one of the female teachers. The audience loved it. At 10-years-old, on a trip to

Disney World, when they asked a volunteer to perform with the singers in the country-western show, my hand was the first to go up. The next thing I knew I was performing with the band! I remember writing a few short stories about Love, Earth and People in the 3rd grade - having it published in the school newsletter and getting recognized for it by my peers. If it meant being front-and-center I was the first to say, 'I'm ready!'

I developed a stutter around the 4th grade and felt many of my "stage" dreams start to slip away – because I lacked the courage to confront my speech demon. I poured myself instead into the craft of writing, because when I wrote what was in my mind I could flow and be free. Since I didn't need to speak, there were no constraints or worry about what I might have to say next and no fear of being unable to communicate because of my speech impediment.

Was I satisfied that I left the creative and performance-driven part of me hiding in the shadows behind my speech impediment? Of course not. But I hid pretty well that I was not satisfied with the path of my life. I compromised; I did not reveal myself, for fear others would not like me, or laugh at me. I still remember not answering questions in class or even providing the wrong answer (a word I knew I could say), because I was afraid I would stutter on the right answer! One of the saddest moments of my teenage life was standing in line, eager to try out for a part in the senior play, *Grease*. As I stood there watching some of my classmates read their lines in front of the director and the others who would decide on the roles in the play, I panicked. Just two people away from my turn to read, I turned around and left the room. I decided I couldn't risk reading aloud if the other students and the director had the script right in front of them - if I stuttered, or left out a word, or changed a word, then everyone would know. I actually walked out, and rationalized I could just work on the lighting crew to still be a part of the show. That never happened either. It was the beginning of the end of any acting opportunities in high school, or college. I never mustered the courage. Instead I returned inward to my writing and became Features and Entertainment editor for my college newspaper. It was cool, but it wasn't all I really wanted. I was unsatisfied with that part of my life.

Eventually, I lined up a college internship at a TV station to be a writer, and life took a turn. There, my surroundings and the attraction to be on TV was too much for me to hide myself any longer. I was hooked and I wanted more. I loved the atmosphere of television and the newsroom; I started as a writer/producer but I wanted to have an on-air role as well. I eventually sought out some private speech therapy, though the therapist said I was hard to treat since I rarely showed I was stuttering. I also got into my own head and told myself, 'I want this so bad I've simply got to go for it.' I ended up earning an on-air producer role, which was unique in the industry, and then got the opportunity to be a feature reporter for the morning show. I fought back against my stutter, learned to pause before words I had trouble saying and I made my dream a reality.

That desire for satisfaction led to a 10-year run on local TV and an Emmy Award for Best News Program in a medium market. I still look back on this time in my life with such fond memories and such satisfaction for what I accomplished. I get to look back with no regrets.

That career was wonderful, but once I started a family the financial and time constraints became too much. So, I sacrificed my dreams to make a better living for my new, growing family and left TV behind to go into sales. I was successful, very, very successful, but internally still unsatisfied. I enjoyed helping people better their insurance situation, but I also knew I had other gifts and talents which were calling me – writing, speaking, inspiring. I could feel it. To move in that direction, I started reading books on inspiration and our human internal conversation. I got up in front of the other agents at some of our weekly meetings, and was able to emotionally articulate about mindset and success in that business and in life (what a joy to do it with my speech impediment in the rear-view mirror). I had the credibility to address the group, since I was one of the most successful agents in the region where I worked. I would receive great feedback from my talks and it validated the reasoning that I was built for more than just the insurance world.

Once I found the power of personal development and self-improvement, I felt a yearning for greater satisfaction in my life more than ever before. I became part of a Mastermind group with three other men who have become like brothers to me; each of us striving to become the best version of ourselves. As I grew and changed, I believed for the better; I was criticized and told to keep it all in check and keep it inside me. No one wanted to hear about a bigger, better life. No one wanted to hear me talk about big dreams, goals, and how I wanted to share my gifts with the world. The world was calling me to become more, but it seemed for the most part I was the only one who could hear it. The revelation of my truest self was sometimes met with disdain and criticism, but despite it all, I knew I was not taking courageous action to be who I was meant to be, the pure and total me, every minute of every day.

The more I acted like "me" the more I felt I was living a life I didn't believe was serving me. Deep inside I was lonely, not satisfied with my existence. I was doing the one thing I never wanted to do – just exist. Just to follow the rules, be a good boy and tip-toe to my grave, with many never even knowing I came this way. If I can't live my purpose, and I cannot share my gifts and bring tremendous value and significance, then what personal legacy have I left behind? My daughters will certainly be my forever legacy, but there can be more, much more. My mission is to positively impact the lives of a billion people. Billion. With a "B." To do this, I had better know who I am and what I want and be satisfied with those parts of me.

The desire for life satisfaction has kept me moving forward with nearly unrelenting drive and purpose. It is not easy; it is hard. But, life is hard.

I now live with the satisfaction that I can build a life by providing value with my gifts and talents that the world desperately needs. A big one is writing stories like this. Our lives are defined by the stories we tell. If you tell good stories, you can literally change the world. I published my first book in September 2013 and it became a #1 Amazon Best Seller. Not "satisfied" with just the book, I started a blog where I write about life, and each Sunday I tell the stories of other people – stories of courage, hope and inspiration. I published my second book in June of this year (2017), and have also launched a storytelling and public speaking/inspiration business. Storytelling is powerful. Life happens in the narratives we tell one another. Data can persuade people, but it doesn't inspire them to act; to do that, you need to wrap your vision in a story that fires the imagination and stirs the soul. That's what great stories do, they attract clients and raving fans, so you don't have to pursue. Your story is uniquely yours. And when you share your challenges or vulnerabilities you give other people permission to do the same. This is at the heart of my Storytelling business.

I also help people change their story. This year I launched an inspirational speaking program called *Lasting Change: Change your story. Change your life.* I show people a few simple habits that, if done consistently over time, will help them change the construct of their lives. What's easy to do is also easy not to do. Changing your life can be easy, it's just hard for many of us to accept it needs to be done.

So the question I ask of you is this – what will make you satisfied? Perhaps you are already living in satisfaction every moment of every day. My guess is you are not, because satisfaction in life is not really a finite point for any of us. For me it's the daily growth, the grind of going out and doing what I need to become the very best version of myself. I need to add tremendous value to other people's lives, by writing, speaking, inspiring, and continuously and consistently working to become more – every single day. If I become more, I have more to give.

It's also the feeling of acceptance and of love from those who are closest to me. Being able to be my true self and to be accepted by someone I care about brings me great satisfaction. The freedom to pursue my dreams and work toward my full potential in life provides me those same feelings – for I know I am here for a reason, actually several reasons – to love, to serve, to care, with all the gifts and talents God presents through me.

If I can feel and live this way - and I am no different in the structure of my human-ness than any of the other 7 billion people on the planet– then, why can't you? Why can't you want more, and why can't you go after more? If you're not satisfied with who you are or where you are – do you understand that in any given moment you already have the power to change? Change your mind and you change your life. Believe it can happen, and should happen, for you. Whatever it is that brings you true joy and satisfaction – focus on that – and never give up on that desire. If you tap into the power of Universal Intelligence, it will follow your lead. You have one life to lead – and only one – so why not be satisfied with all you have to give and the life that you live?

I wish to inspire and change the world – on a course to the same destination to which we all are going at some point in time, the end of our time on this earth. Perhaps on my gravestone I will have a few words inscribed which allow me to rest in peace. Words I believe that could work for any of us: Love. Legacy. Satisfaction.

* * * * *

A Husband, a Wife and a Waffle Maker

Nancy Ward

In the fall of 1995, after graduating college with a degree in marketing, I moved from Ohio to Virginia and got a job designing marketing materials for Kinko's. I enjoyed desktop publishing and marketing, and this was my first pre-corporate job after college. Unfortunately, the job didn't satisfy my entrepreneurial spirit. I wanted to have a business of my own to help people, and ended up starting my own desktop publishing business. In January of 1997, I found myself at a trade show looking for new clients, and stopped at the Pampered Chef booth. I had never heard of the company, but was familiar with the direct sales industry. For $99, I could become a consultant, learn how to cook, make money showing guests how to use the cooking tools, help others start their own business, and even earn trips with the company. I had nothing to lose; my desktop publishing business wasn't doing all that well, and I still had that drive to be an entrepreneur. I remember thinking: *This might be just what I'm looking for.*

The following year, I moved back to Ohio and started accumulating debt on my credit cards that I wasn't able to pay off each month. I debated if I should try to continue running my business or just quit. I wasn't much of a quitter; if I decided to throw in the towel, I would feel guilty about leaving the company. Even though I didn't know anyone in the area, that fall I restarted my business. I rented a booth at a children's themed trade show and talked to everyone who stopped by. Many moms filled out the prize drawing slip, providing me their name and number – they were interested in hosting a party. Over the next two weeks, I made phone calls every night, booking shows and filling up my fall calendar. I felt confident, successful and on fire.

Because I worked my business night after night, that year I earned a trip to New Orleans and a nice paycheck, just from selling kitchen tools. The next two years were very busy, as I worked hard and earned trips to Munich, Germany and Miami, Florida. Then, in the fall of 2001, I met the man who would become my husband. I wanted to spend my weekends with him instead of holding shows, so of course I saw my business fall off significantly. We dated for a few years and eventually married in 2004.

My husband didn't like to have debt hanging around – he was co-owner of a company and had a great income. Within a few years of being married, my $40,000 of credit card debt was gone. For years after that, I was living a wealthy life. I had what every little girl dreams about – a husband, children, a house, no worries over bills and even trips to Disney World and Disneyland with the family. Within four years of being married, we had paid off our house. Life was good.

At times, I still felt guilty about the debt I brought into our marriage, and wanted my income to help with the bills. My husband kept telling me that I should do the Pampered Chef shows just for fun, and not make it serious. My job was to, "Focus on being Mom first, instead of the business." As much as I understood that, I think there is something that some men just don't realize: the need for women, especially mothers, to be appreciated and have something of their own. I was proud to go to shows, be on my game, and bring home a nice commission; the free products I earned were a nice bonus as well. But my business wasn't important to my husband: he didn't appreciate even the smallest accomplishments I made. He never encouraged me, like a spouse should. No "Go get 'em, have fun, and do your best." He always seemed to have a pessimistic or condescending comment, especially on the nights I came home from a show with a low sales amount.

When our daughter was born, I was fortunate enough to stay home with her instead of having to work a full-time job. The only downfall to that was being a stay-at-home mom was exhausting both mentally and physically. But, no one gets a gold star for doing the laundry or dishes. I continued to hold Pampered Chef parties as a way for me to have "me" time and something to keep me motivated. I enjoyed the recognition of my peers and the company for the sales that I brought in. Unfortunately, I felt unsupported at home.

My husband would arrive home after work, have dinner, and immediately head to the basement to his woodshop to work on his woodturning hobby. As much as I loved motherhood, I also was tired of being "on" 24/7 and needed a break from time to time. He still considered my business to be a "hobby", and therefore on par with his own. Once, after a lot of time working in the basement on a project for the next contest, he must have had a twinge of guilt; he gave me a $150 gift certificate to a local salon so I could get a massage or haircut. It wasn't money that I wanted. I wanted some of his time, attention, and acknowledgment that what I was doing was important.

While pregnant with our son a year later, I again caught the bug to do more in my business. I booked parties on the weekends, knowing that my husband would be able to take care of our one-year-old daughter. Within a few months, I started to get a lot of grief from him about how much time I was away from the house. Keep in mind, I was still home during the day with our daughter, cooking, cleaning, doing laundry. I guess I felt a bit defiant, and didn't let that stop me; I actually ramped it up more. That year I worked so much, it was the fourth best-selling year I had since my early, trip-earning years of my business. I had to pat myself on the back, because my husband wasn't going to.

As with any of us, we try to get through our days the best we can. I wasn't sure how to change myself or my husband to make things better. I was absorbed in Mom duties and my business, and probably neglecting my relationship with my husband. As the years went by, it got more and more tense, and we were less and less of a team.

It was the little things I noticed, that made me realize change needed to happen. For example, when we went to holiday events for our kids, he wouldn't have any conversation or interaction with me. He just seemed bored, and at one event he was on the phone the entire time. When I confronted him about it, he just said the kids weren't doing anything exciting. But we weren't there for our own entertainment, we were there to be a family and enjoy the moments. As a parent, we are supposed to support our children, even if their activities don't interest us. Some of those memories mean the world to our kids.

In the summer of 2012, I wanted to take a trip to Louisville to sightsee and visit the museums with our kids. I planned it during the week, so we could avoid the crowds. When I asked my husband to take a few days off work and join us, he said it would be too boring and if he was going to take time off, he would rather have those few days in the woodshop instead. We went without him and had a fantastic time. For many years we took separate vacations; he went to woodturning conferences and classes, and I went to scrapbooking events and vacations with our kids. That should have been a sign; no healthy couple takes vacations without each other. We were certainly going in different directions.

Things were still tense the following year, and we were both seeing our own therapists to work on being better parents, not necessarily to be a better couple. He planned a 40th birthday party for me, the first time he had ever done more than dinner with the family for my birthday. But, during the party we were never in the same room together. If I was outside, he was inside, and vice versa. Around that time, I had started on a simple weight loss plan, and bought my own bike and accessories for myself for my birthday. I was losing weight and proud of myself for it. For my birthday, he got me a waffle maker.

By the fall, we were going to marriage counseling to try to fix us, since we were still having issues working together with our kids. Both of my kids have ADHD, and for the past five years, there had been a lot of tension in our house. We didn't agree on parenting styles, or much of anything else. My husband continually lost his patience with our kids, was condescending to them, and from time to time was unnecessarily forcing them to do things they didn't want to, which lead to tantrums and crying.

I devoted much of my time and energy to my business and volunteering. At one point, I held 11 positions at the same time – school, PTO, Girl Scouts, and gymnastics boosters; all which required meetings and events out of the house. These things kept me occupied and gave me purpose. It's possible I over-volunteered because I needed a break from the kids, but it's also possible I needed a break from my husband. We got to a point where I would take one night off, and he would take another night off. We weren't often in the house at the same time. Things didn't seem to work when both parents were involved while putting the kids to bed.

The more time went by and the longer it went on, the farther we drifted apart. At a certain point, I acknowledged that if I didn't get out, I would never have that happiness, safety and security of my kids. Money isn't always everything. I knew things were not ever going to turn around, and in December of 2013, we agreed that the only thing we could do was get a divorce. Sadly, for Christmas that year, he didn't buy me a single gift – not any from him, or from the kids. The kids figured out later that Mommy didn't get any gifts.

On January 31, eight months after I started my weight loss plan, I had officially lost 45 pounds. He never let me know he had noticed or complemented me, but I was darn proud of my accomplishment and the strength it took to do it during those troubled times.

By May, he moved into an apartment and in February of 2015, our divorce was final. He got the waffle maker. I had never even used it; even though it was my birthday gift, he bought it so he could make waffles for the kids.

I gave up a lot of money, including a nice IRA, but gained the strength and confidence to make it work as a single mom. I had to make it work, I had no choice. I was the one who wanted a divorce, and I had to own up to my new future. Thankfully, I was able to keep the house, since there would be no way that a single mom, with essentially no income, could rent an apartment. The job market is really tough for stay-at-home moms who need to return to work. Many companies don't seem to want to take a chance on a group of women who are mostly college educated, have a strong work ethic, and want to contribute to the workforce. I started working with a life coach, to make sure I was going in the right direction for my future. Luckily, just like in other times of my life, I still had my Pampered Chef business to fall back on. I controlled my own income. The more shows I did, and the more people I helped start their own businesses, the more money I made. I made a choice to work as hard as I could, working more hours on my business, to create the income that would be able to support me and my kids.

I am still working hard to get post-divorce debt paid off and support my kids. I work at the school as a substitute, I teach online courses about cooking and card making (a suggestion from my life coach), and continue to hold Pampered Chef parties. All these part-time pockets of income are my main streams of income besides child support and the alimony that won't go on forever.

I had wanted the kids to live with me, so they could be on a good schedule with their ADHD, and be away from his house as much as possible. Unfortunately, I didn't win that battle: we have a shared parenting agreement where he has them two nights a week, I have them two nights, and we split up the weekends. The times I spend with my kids when they are at my house, is more meaningful and positive. I encourage them to do things out of their comfort zones, to be proud of their accomplishments and continue to applaud their successes. They have also come to understand that everyone needs a helping hand, to be appreciated, and that sometimes a simple hug can mean the world to a person. Every once in a while, my son will mention that "we shouldn't buy or do that, we need to save money." Bless his heart.

Things have certainly changed a lot in the last 5 years, and many people have asked me if I regret the divorce. For the first few months I did, especially when I missed the money. For example, when the windows in my house needed to be replaced, a $360 per month payment just wasn't in the budget. I kept asking myself: *Why did I do it?* But, then I would notice the tension between us was still there, and I would see the signs of us not being a team while raising our kids. When I look at a family picture we took for a Christmas card, I can still see the "sit down, sit still" words he grunted through his smile – and I know I made the right choice to end the marriage.

Over time, we've learned ways to better work with our kids, we keep a balanced schedule for them, and hardly have disagreements anymore over decisions we make regarding them. Last year, he even moved into his own house, just two miles away from mine. When they ask, still to this day, "Would you get back together?" I can be sure my answer is "No."

After 20 years of selling Pampered Chef, my "why" for the business is 180° difference from when I started. In 1997, I did it for extra money; in 2017, I do it for my children, my house, new windows and health insurance payments. It is still my escape to talk with adults, I get to teach and coach others on how to prepare meals, and I am appreciated by my customers (some who have become great friends), my kids and my team. You ask if I am still living a wealthy life, you bet! I'm in control of my happiness, health, time and money. The relationship with my children is better than before. I am grateful for my new "wealth."

Blinded by the Light

Mike Davis

It's the afternoon of March 3, 2017. I'm seated onstage in Las Vegas. Seated next to me are four of the most influential people in my life. I'm feeling a combination .of elation, excitement.... and fear. These are World Champions, highly successful professional speakers. More than that, they are my mentors, my coaches — people I've idolized for years.

A little voice in my head says: *Don't screw this up, dude.*

The spotlights shining on the stage are adding to the pressure. They are so hot that I can feel the sweat rolling down my back. They're so blinding I have to look away from the audience.

I briefly lock eyes with Darren LaCroix, one of the four champions. My mind travels back to the time when I met him.

He had just won the World Championship of Public Speaking. I was in awe of the man, not just his title. I was mesmerized by his physical style. I was enthralled by his impact on the audience. I was inspired by his ability to make them laugh while he imparted a meaningful message.

I wanted to elicit that same response from my audiences.

We became friends, and he took on the role of mentor.

One day in 2003, he called and said, "Several of the Champs are starting a new group - The Champions Edge. We're designing it to help people become better speakers. We'd like you to be one of our first members."

I was happy he was personally asking me. I said, "Sure, I'd love to join." After I hung up the phone, another idea popped into my head. *I don't want to be a member - I want to be one of the coaches. I want to do what they're doing!*

My next thought sent me down a path that would impact me for the next fourteen years....

If I want to be one of those coaches, I need to do what they've all done - win the World Championship of Public Speaking.

Thus, began my pursuit of the title.

The annual World Championship of Public Speaking is conducted by Toastmasters International. Think of it as *American Idol* for speakers. It's a six-round competition. 30,000 Toastmasters begin; and from the final round of ten participants, one person is crowned World Champion of Public Speaking.

In my first year of competition, I made it to the fifth round. I was one of the last ninety speakers to survive. Even though I didn't advance to the final round, I thought: *That's not bad for a first try. I've got this! Soon enough, I'll be a World Champion and I'll be part of the coaching team.*

Over the following thirteen years, I never again realized the same level of contest success.

In recent years, my results grew worse and worse. I developed a habit of finishing second at earlier levels of the contest each year. At the rate I was going, I figured when I walk into the opening round of the next contest, members will meet me at the door and say, "Here's your Second-Place trophy. Don't bother competing!"

As the years passed, an inner voice grew louder and louder. It said things like: *You're not that good!* and *Who do you think you are?* and *See! The judges can tell you're nowhere near as good as you think. Give it up!*

This voice was slowly eating at my self-confidence. I spoke less and less, thinking: *What's the use? It's never gonna happen.*

However, during those years of contest failure, I had become fascinated with speech coaching. The genesis of this came from a man named Lance Miller. He was the 2005 World Champion of Public Speaking.

Ironically, his title just reaffirmed my belief that to become a Champions Edge coach, I needed to win the World Championship. He had been invited to become one of the coaches after his victory.

The day I met him, I asked, "If you were starting over, what one action would you take to become a better speaker?"

Without hesitation, he said, "Become a better speech evaluator. Learn how to find the good in others' speeches, as well as areas for improvement. Your speeches will naturally become better just by evaluating others."

Since Lance had achieved something I was striving for, I followed his advice. For the next 18 months, I rarely gave any speeches, but I evaluated every speaker I could find. I reviewed videos of speeches, speakers in person, and speakers on TV.

My work paid off. I became a very good evaluator. So much so that other people started asking me for feedback. Others wanted me to coach them. They were thrilled with my feedback.

In 2011, I completed the Certified World Class Speech Coaching certification. This program was facilitated by World

Champion speaker Craig Valentine. He became another of my speaking mentors.

In that same year, I started my own company, Speaking CPR. People were now paying me to do something I love.

And my work was noticed by others. On a warm spring Tuesday in 2013, I received a call at 1:30 in the afternoon. "Michael, it's Darren LaCroix. Can you be in Baltimore Thursday morning?"

I said, "Why would I want to do that?"

"Craig just blew out his knee playing basketball. He can't lead the Storytelling workshop with me. We talked about it, and you're our first choice to take his place."

I thought, 'Wow, how cool!'

After quickly adjusting my calendar for the rest of the week, I called Darren back and said, "I'm in. I'll be in Baltimore Thursday."

During my flight to Baltimore, I was excited. What an opportunity! I still felt the same on the cab ride to the hotel and while I was checking in.

When I arrived at the meeting room the next morning, my inner voice loudly said: *What are you thinking? You think you're as good as Darren and Craig? These guys are so far ahead of you. I don't know what you said to fool them, but, you don't belong here.*

A feeling of dread washed over me.

What WAS I thinking?

I wasn't an accomplished speaker like these guys - my speaking heroes. They'd done so much, and I had done so little. Or so I thought.

For the first couple hours of the workshop, I said very little. I quietly stood at the front of the room with Darren. The attendees were there to see Darren and Craig, not Darren and Michael.

It didn't take Darren long to sense my apprehension. At one point, while coaching one of the attendees, he said, "Mike, I'm not sure what Natalie should do. What do you think?"

I was caught off guard. I didn't have time to be nervous, he wanted an answer.

I gave him - and Natalie - feedback on her speech. When I finished, she said, "I really like those ideas. Thanks, Mike."

Darren said, "Nice advice. It's about time you spoke up in here." Everyone in the room, including me, burst out into laughter. It was just the break in tension I needed.

The rest of the event was a success. Darren and Craig were grateful for my contributions. Natalie even hired ME for one-on-one coaching after that workshop!

I'll always be grateful to Darren for "throwing me into the fire" when he did. It was exactly what I needed to gain my confidence.

Two years after the Baltimore workshop, Darren asked me to help out with his newly created University - Stage Time University - in various capacities.

Despite all my coaching successes, there was a nagging feeling that never left me. That little voice that reminded me: *You're not a World Champion. You're not as good as them. You'll never be as good as them.*

That message was still part of the background noise in my brain when Darren called me in January of 2017. "Mike, I want you to be the emcee for Lady and the Champs this year."

Lady and the Champs is an annual event held in Las Vegas. It features Hall of Fame and World Champion speakers, Las Vegas headliners, world renowned speech coaches, and a leading Hollywood screenwriting consultant.

It's a Big Deal!

And I was just asked to be the emcee for all three days.

Which is why I am on stage on March 3, sitting next to my mentors, looking away from that blinding light. I'm not just the emcee - I'm also coaching attendees. Alongside my heroes.

And that's when a new voice pops into my head. It starts out as a whisper, but quickly grows louder....

Hey!

You made it!

You're on stage with your heroes. You're one of the coaches at Stage Time. You're one of THEM.

A shiver shoots up and down my spine.

My eyes get misty.

It happens quickly, and I have to maintain composure - I'm the emcee, after all. But the feeling in that moment is seared into my memory.

I'm a coach, just like the people I've looked up to for years. They're treating me like an equal, because I have earned the right to be there.

Since that event, and through many discussions with the people who were there, I realize the significance of the blinding light shining onto that stage. For a decade and a half, I was blinded by the titles, trophies and accolades that my mentors had won. I fooled myself into believing it was the only path to my goal of coaching with them.

The lesson I learned was that they aren't World Champions because they're great speakers; they are World Champions because they are authentic, they are willing to share their stories, and they are true to who they are.

And that's why I've been accepted as one them. I deserve to be there because I've been most authentic as a speech coach.

To this point, it's not been my destiny to be a World Champion. Maybe someday it will be. Or maybe it won't. It no longer defines me.

Today, I approach every coaching and speaking opportunity with a new perspective and new confidence. I have much to offer, and I'm living my dream when I get to do both.

As you pursue your greatest aspirations, don't make the mistake I made. Don't be blinded. Be true to yourself, take advantage of opportunities, and you just might realize your greatest dream. Just not the way you expected.

* * * * *

Escape from the Law

Kwame Christian

There are a lot of legal escapees. People who have made the transition from the law to other professions, because the practice of law is very conservative. Not conservative in the political sense; but in a risk-aversion sense. That's our job – our job is to worry about our clients and think about the worst possible things that could happen, so it's very rare to see people who are very entrepreneurial be lawyers. If you want to escape, you'll need to become comfortable with the fact that your risk-averse friends will be questioning your decisions and they'll be questioning your sanity. They'll also be questioning your ability, because they will assume the only reason you choose not to be a lawyer is you couldn't cut it. I think that could be said of people in almost every profession, but that was one of the things that held me back. I worried: *What are my lawyer friends going to think if I stop practicing law?*

But I just had to realize that first, these people are not actually talking to me; I'm assuming that these are the negative things that they're saying, and that might not even be real. And second, if they're thinking these things, they're not my friends. So why am I trying to concern myself with people who don't care about me? I just had to decide that I would feel better with my life if I failed my way than if I succeeded somebody else's way. Coming to that realization gave me a lot more liberty and confidence to change gears.

I told myself: *Listen, whether I win or lose, I'm doing this my way and I'm going to enjoy it.*

I couldn't face the prospect of being stuck in a career where I could make a lot of money, but feel unfulfilled and be upset.

That was not a life I was willing to live. To me following the path of least resistance versus possibly living out my dreams, was an easy choice to make once I started thinking about it that way.

My name is Kwame Christian and I am a legal escapee. I am now the Director of the American Negotiation Institute. I also host a weekly podcast that teaches business professionals how to be more persuasive. I came up with the idea of the American Negotiation Institute by following my passion. I love negotiating and resolving disputes and I love teaching these skills to others.

The way I found negotiation in law school was that the class fit into my schedule. That's the only reason I took the class. I didn't have any idea that I would enjoy it. I was just going through the motions at the time.

I was thinking to myself: *I don't like law and I just figured that out. What do I do now?*

I found this class that fit into my schedule and I thought: *Let's do it.*

I'm so glad I did. It was so cool, because it was easily the most practical thing I have ever learned in school. I could see how it works with lawyers. Because 95% of cases settle; settle meaning they negotiate it out before you get to see the trial. So, lawyers are negotiating all the time. And in business, people are negotiating all the time. When you have a broad perspective of what negotiating is you realize you're negotiating all the time at home with your spouse, your family and your friends. This was the most important thing I could ever learn.

I didn't know it when I signed up for the class, but it turned out that Ohio State had the 2nd highest ranked Dispute

Resolution program in the country (now it is number one); ahead of Harvard, Yale, Stanford, all of those prestigious schools. It's a very highly acclaimed program and they had a negotiation competition after the class. You pick a partner, and are given these prompts to negotiate on behalf of your fictional clients. Judges, mediators and lawyers in the community judge your performance and tell you how well you did.

When I heard about it, I thought: *That will be fun! Let's do it.*

And so, my partner and I won the competition at our school, which gave us the opportunity to represent the school at the American Bar Association's regional competition in Ottawa, Ontario. And then we won that competition, too. We then represented the school at the national competition in New Orleans, Louisiana and made it to the semi-finals there. I was hooked.

I was thinking: *Whatever I do in life, it needs to involve this.* And that's when the love affair with negotiation began.

I realized that the key to my success in the negotiation competition wasn't that I knew more than other people; I had just taken the one class. The key was the fact that I became obsessed with this. My partner and I simply outworked the competition. We outworked everybody. A negotiation is won in the preparation, not the implementation. If you prepare the right way, your performance is almost a forgone conclusion. It was really the preparation that set us apart. You might be smarter than me, you might be better looking than me, but you will not outwork me. Especially not in this field; I have too much passion and curiosity, and I will simply work harder than other people because I like it.

My basic training in negotiation started in my youth. Fitting in was my silent struggle. As a first-generation Caribbean

American living in small town Ohio, I was always racially, ethnically, and culturally different from my classmates. I looked different and when I spoke, I sounded different. This made it difficult for me to connect with my peers. At a young age, I learned that I had to take the first steps of friendship in order to make connections. Looking back on those days with a critical, academic lens, it is clear to me that these were my first negotiations. I was negotiating friendship. I was negotiating acceptance.

I remember one day in first grade going on the playground and being rejected at every turn. There were different groups of people playing different games and for some reason that day I was unable to gain acceptance to any of the groups. I remember coming back into the classroom crying and the teacher made an announcement to the class saying that the children needed to be more friendly and inclusive. After this hurtful experience, I vowed to do whatever it took to be accepted by my peers. I promised that this would never happen again, and it didn't.

What's funny about this story is that if I were to tell my friends from grade school or high school about the story they not only wouldn't remember it, but they probably wouldn't believe me. Throughout elementary school, middle and high school, I was always the popular person. I had the rare kind of popularity that was easily transferable. My differences really made me keenly aware of my surroundings and forced me to focus on building rapport and being liked. I could eat lunch one day with the jocks, the next with the members of the band, a third day with the international exchange students, and I could transfer seamlessly between these groups like a chameleon. I knew everyone in the school by name and greeted each of them as I walked through the halls. This background became the foundation of one of the most powerful tools in my arsenal of persuasion: the ability to gain trust and acceptance.

Right after I graduated from law school, I was working at a public policy research institute. After about a year, I decided that I would open my own law firm to specifically serve the needs of entrepreneurs. I started to build up the firm on the side while still working full-time doing policy work. The whole time I was building up the law firm I knew that this was just a temporary fix because my ultimate goal was to do something related to negotiation. However, since I didn't know the path forward at the time, I started the law firm because I knew it would give me the opportunity to negotiate and develop more experience.

I was able to build up enough business with my firm to leave my job at the policy institute in February of 2016 and pursue the law firm full-time. This was when I had my first major breakthrough on my path to success. I had always thought that I would have to practice law for 5 to 10 years before I would be "qualified enough" to serve as a negotiation consultant. After spending some time in introspection, I knew I had to challenge that assumption. I decided to create the American Negotiation Institute and build that consulting firm while building the law firm. That came to be the best business decision of my life.

My strategy with the Institute was to focus first on building my reputation and exposure in the business community. To do that, I launched a weekly podcast that teaches business professionals how to be more persuasive. The name of my company is the American Negotiation Institute. I must have been feeling very creative and original when I launched the podcast, because I named it the *American Negotiation Institute's Podcast.* So, obviously that had to change. I don't think many people know about the original name, because I'm just not sure there were many people listening. I changed it to *Negotiation for Entrepreneurs*, since that was the target market I wanted to approach. Hosting a podcast is tough in the beginning, because you are talking to yourself, and trying to be interesting. You don't know if anyone is listening. I wanted to know who was listening, so I started surveying the listeners via Linked-In. I found out only about 34% of my listeners are entrepreneurs. And when I looked at the stats of my episodes, I found the episodes that focused on career, or the general episodes like the car negotiation, or the holiday gift-giving guide, or the episode on how to say no effectively, those are my most popular episodes.

So, I sent out another survey, that basically said, "You people are not who I thought you were, but that's cool. Tell me what you want to hear, and I will talk about those things."

And, since most of my listeners weren't entrepreneurs, I thought we needed a new name. I asked them to tell me what they wanted the new name of the podcast to be. So, it was put to a vote, and they actually chose a name that I never would have chosen myself. But the name that was overwhelmingly the most popular was *Negotiate Anything*. So that's the new name. The response has been overwhelming! After only eight months, the show is now the top ranked negotiation podcast on iTunes, was featured on the homepage of iTunes, and has listeners in over 60 different countries.

When you are starting a blog or a podcast you have to become comfortable with the fact that you will be talking to yourself for the first few months, and that can be incredibly discouraging. However, it's important to recognize that people aren't willing to commit to you until you show that you are willing to commit to yourself. Most podcasts end after six episodes because the host simply couldn't keep up. He or she got discouraged and quit. If somebody sees that you are constantly producing content they feel comfortable committing to you because they know you won't leave them.

My podcast brought me my first and most memorable client. He's a lawyer who listened to the podcast, and he sent me this long email explaining a scenario that he was dealing with. He said he loved the podcast, explained the situation, said he worked in the legal field, but was not particularly good at negotiations, and he'd like to bring me in as a consultant. What do you think my reaction was when I first read the email? Excitement? Dollar signs?

No. I thought: *This is a scam, this can't be real. Nobody's even listening to this podcast, I'm here talking to myself.*

But then I thought: *His English is solid, he's using a lot of legal terms appropriately, I'll send a polite email back just in case.*

He replied with, "Let's have a call and chat."

It turned out this guy was 100% legit – he wanted my help on a multi-million-dollar deal. He was in a situation where his client owed 4 different people, and there was about 1.5 million dollars to go around. The parties his client owed wanted a total of 3.4 million. That math does not work. So, he wanted me to come in as a consultant and help him out. And then, the dollar signs started going off. We've been working together on a number of cases since. We were able to get a deal in that impossible case, so since then whenever he has tough cases he reaches out to me, and he's referred friends to me too. It's been a really interesting part of the business. I never thought of myself as somebody who could be brought in as a negotiation consultant. Not because I didn't think I had the skills, but because I didn't know there was a business opportunity there. But when you put yourself out there, opportunities will find you. That has been a lot of fun; we've had some interesting cases together.

My biggest regret was doubting myself for so long, and that it took so long to pursue this path. Creating a podcast was something that I always wanted to do. I was always passionate about teaching people how to negotiate. A podcast was the obvious option and I failed to pursue it for years because I didn't think I was good enough. Self-doubt can cripple execution. One of my favorite sayings as an entrepreneur is "fail faster." Failure is going to happen. We need to embrace it, learn from it, make the necessary adjustments and try again. The number one characteristic of successful entrepreneurs is grit - the resolve to push through obstacles and dedication to a singular goal.

Let me give you an example of where I failed and learned. I think this is an example of trying to push too hard. My client was trying to sell their property. I was asked to consult in the middle of this multi-million-dollar real estate deal. Unfortunately, I was in a situation where I didn't know the entire relationship dynamic between my client and the other party. I wasn't aware that my client was dragging their feet when it came to getting things in order, taking a long time to respond, and so the other party was getting frustrated. They were questioning my client's commitment to the deal. We were at the point where the deal was already made, but we needed to decide which expenses were going to be paid by who. There was an $8,000 expense that they asked my client to pay. They didn't substantiate the amount; they didn't say why they wanted $8,000 or why they thought my client should pay it, they just wanted $8,000. This is a multi-million-dollar deal, so $8,000 in the grand scheme of things is not that much. But, I wanted to get as much value as I could for my client. I said, since they didn't substantiate it, we could split the difference; it obviously wasn't important. So, by pushing for just that little bit more, the other party decided to just walk away from the deal. That was a mistake because I asked for more without really considering the relationship dynamics. They didn't trust my client's commitment to the deal. That and the fact that we were willing to push on such a minor issue, made them feel we weren't really committed and so they walked away. I feel bad about it, but I think given the totality of circumstances and seeing what my clients did in subsequent interactions, they probably would have walked away for another infraction. But I know in that case it was because I pushed too hard. I have learned from that to take everything into consideration and not get too greedy. If it's a good deal, take it, it's not worth the risk pushing too far.

It was exciting and it's good to learn. The way I look at it when it comes to career advancement or even just life, if all you do is win, win, win no matter what; it means you're not trying very hard. It means you're not pushing yourself. It was a loss, and it did hurt, but I think it's supposed to hurt. That's how it sticks, so you can pick yourself up, learn from it and not make the same mistake again.

The first step in becoming a better negotiator is getting comfortable with the ask. That's where most negotiations end, because people forget to ask for what they want. They're too afraid, they don't want to seem needy, they don't want to seem greedy, and they don't want to hurt people's feelings. But you need to get over it. Engage in rejection therapy. Ask for things that you think you'll never get. Negotiate for a discount next time you're getting your car repaired. When I go to the coffee shop, I ask for extra pastries. My heart flutters every time, like it's a big deal even though I do this almost every day. Remember, courage is not acting without fear, it's acting in spite of fear. Negotiating those small things will make you more emotionally prepared when it's time to negotiate the big things. Don't sleep on those opportunities – negotiate everything. Or, as in the name of my podcast, go ahead and Negotiate Anything.

The most important thing you can do to improve your ability to persuade is not focus so much on what you say, but what you ask and then listening to the response. When you negotiate the right way, your breakdown of conversation should be about 70-30, where the other side is talking and you are listening 70% of the time, and you're only speaking 30%. When you achieve that breakdown, that means you're asking great questions, which means you're getting more information, which makes you a more competent negotiator. And what you'll find is sometimes if you ask the right questions, you can lead people down a logical path where they persuade themselves without you making any affirmative statements. So, the best thing you can do; be more curious, ask more, great open-ended questions.

Currency and Change

Karynne Summars

"At first glance, it may appear too hard. Look again. Always look again."

~ Mary Ann Radmacher

As a student in elementary school, I received an assignment to write inspirational quotes in my fellow students' journals. These quotes had to be meaningful and guide the students toward a goal, as well as inspire them to do well in life. I enjoyed this writing task and put a lot of thought into it before I put pen to paper.

Before email communication existed, I also enjoyed writing letters to my friends and family, going into great detail to describe my travel experiences and other activities. I often enhanced these with a suitable cutout from a magazine, or photos I had taken, to provide a visual aid.

Despite these early signs, at that time I had no idea that I would one day be writing novels, a personal development book, and screenplays. I loved to read and often admired the way the writers told their stories that pulled me in and allowed me to envision them like movies in my mind. When I watched a movie that had been adapted from a book I had read, I was often disappointed. The book was so much better than the movie. It seemed that the author of a book could take you much deeper into the story, and I eventually learned the reason why. A screenplay should not be longer than 120 pages and the screenwriter must come to the point quickly in order to move the story forward.

Later in life, while working as a corporate finance professional, I prepared board presentations for the deals I was pursuing. The decision to complete a transaction could be based on what I had written, and I always kept that in mind. I made sure to be very clear, describing the transactions thoroughly. While I was working in finance, I always felt that something was missing in my life. To satisfy my creative side I started to create storybooks for colleagues who were leaving our bank with the title: *This Was Your Life at* _____. My storybooks would describe their experiences at work and related stories, as well as our friendship. I also used photos I had taken over the years to show and tell. These storybooks became quite popular and I enjoyed creating them.

About four years ago I had the urge to write a book, but wasn't sure if I would be able to finish an entire novel. I was concerned about the time commitment involved in a full-length novel and what to do with potential writer's block. I decided to start with a couple of pages to see where it would lead. I was amazed at how easily the material was flowing without any signs of writer's block. I often wrote until 2:00 a.m., although I had to get up by 6:30 a.m. again to get ready for work.

Soon, I realized that this was what had been missing in my life—my love for storytelling, entertaining readers and touching them emotionally. It had become very clear that I had to follow my passion for writing. The challenge now was to find the time to write and finish the novel I had started. A couple of years after the world financial crisis had hit I left the finance industry to focus on my creative talent. I just realized that with the changed business climate and not being able to get certain finance deals approved anymore, it would be best to focus on my writing instead of spinning my wheels on deals that would not get approved anyway. Within seven months I had finished my first novel, *Desperate Pursuit in Venice*, and

I am currently working on the second edition. Today, I can honestly say I am living my dream.

They say that you should write about what you know, and so I did. Setting the story in beautiful international locations delivered a perfect setting and mood for the storyline. I could describe my favorite places in perfect detail, which allowed my readers to virtually travel there and live vicariously through the captivating characters I created.

While I was writing my first novel, I experienced all kinds of emotions. I laughed, I cried and I was proud of my female main character. Writing the sequel gave me the opportunity to create new situations, thrilling and emotional in the extreme, which allowed the antagonist to redeem himself in the end and thus creating a happy ending for all concerned.

This sequel puts the protagonist in harm's way while pursuing another important acquisition. While I was writing the story, I was watching the World Soccer Championships play out in Brazil, and this beautiful country is on my bucket list of places to visit. Since I had not yet been to Brazil, I had to do far more research for this novel. It was extremely educational, as I had to learn a lot about the perils in the rainforest. During this research, I became emotionally involved in the subject of deforestation of rainforests and I decided to dedicate this book to the indigenous tribes in the Amazon rainforests and their quest to preserve our green planet.

This is not where my writing journey ends, however. I have moved on to also write the screenplay inspired by my first novel. I was forced to eliminate several subplots from my book, which did not move the main plot forward as is required for a film. I loved the process of adapting my own book to a screenplay; it gave me the opportunity to condense it to the important parts about the main characters. It actually propelled me into focusing on screenplays, rather than writing more novels. This is just another way I have reinvented myself once again.

Since then I have written another screenplay with a co-writer about the troubled childhood, rise to stardom and eventual friendship of two American icons. My next screenplay is an espionage thriller set in Berlin during the time the wall was separating East and West Germany, which is inspired by true events. My non-fiction personal development book will also be published in 2017. It is designed to give people of all ages the tools to transform their life.

I love my life as a writer and I am grateful to have received the gifts of storytelling and mentoring others from the universe.

The catalyst for all of this was the financial crisis in 2008, which resulted in the demise of various banks and businesses. With that, business as I knew it changed and catapulted me in the direction of leaving the financial industry to focus on my writing journey. It also led me to joining film projects at a producer level or collaborating with filmmakers on various levels.

What's the moral of this story? Simply, that there is a silver lining in every cloud. When you face adversity, you must stay strong and focused and be ready for change. In the process, you may actually find your true passion and calling.

All She Wanted Was a Brick House

Leroy Reshard

I was born in 1945, to a 21-year-old single mother in Tallahassee, Florida. When I was born my brother was almost 4 years old. Two years later we gained a sister, and then another brother came along in 1951. Now my mother had four children by four different sorry men. We all lived in one room of my grandparents' home on their small family farm. Our mother was a strong, loving and hard-working woman. She did domestic work six days a week so we could eat and have clothes to wear. She loved her children and her family very much. We went to church on a regular basis and we believed in Jesus. My mother taught me and all her children to go to school, get an education and learn. She wanted a better life for us than she had. She taught us to love people, work hard in school and on the farm and dream.

Going to school and listening to other children talking about fishing and hunting with their dads made me feel bad. So, my brother and I began to call our granddaddy...Daddy! My grandparents had 12 children and all of them were married, except for my mother. I often wondered why she never married, and I still do at times. When we were young, my brother and I use to argue about which of our dads she should have married. He always said his dad and I always said mine. When I got older and learned who a Dad actually is...I realized none of them were worthy of us.

Our home was a loving home. We loved each other, and the white folks my mother worked for loved us too. They would give us clothes from their children and we wore them with pride. I learned to love all people because we got so much from the folks she worked for. We were very happy kids growing up in the country.

Rural Tallahassee was segregated during the 1950's and 60's. Going to segregated schools was fine for a while. Our school books were used hand me down books from the white schools. Our teachers loved us and encouraged us to learn, learn, and learn because they knew what was ahead of us. Our teachers were awesome! When I moved on to our segregated high school in town, I realized that many of the children living in town were smarter and they lived better than we did. We were all very proud and we didn't have to deal with race issues.

My mother worked hard to support her children. We all worked on the family farm growing corn, cotton, okra, and vegetables to sell. We also grew greens, okra, cucumbers, and corn in our family garden and raised chickens and hogs. My older brother and I went fishing and hunting and ate what we caught. We never missed a meal.

Almost daily, my mother prayed for a brick house so we could have place of our own. Every summer we would take our corn, cotton and okra to sell at the mill and every year it wasn't enough money to buy a brick house. It was barely enough to help buy food and clothes for school. We were just poor and living without electricity or plumbing in one room in her parent's home.

But, when I was in the second grade, we moved into a two-room house. It felt good to rent our very own house and have our very own garden. It still wasn't a brick house, but it was something we had worked for.

I didn't realize how poor we were until I moved from Tallahassee to Hempstead, New York after graduating from high school in 1963. I had come to New York looking for a better life and job. With only a high school education in

Tallahassee, there were not many opportunities. In New York, I got a job as an electrician in an all-white company in Levittown. While wiring houses all over Long Island, I was in a world I had not seen before. I realized we were poor! I was only 18 years old, and my first full year as an electrician I made $3,000. I said, "Lord just let make $10,000 a year, and I will be on top of the world!"

Two years later, I was drafted by the US Army. Wow...What an awesome experience. I served in Vietnam for 18 months and really matured to be a solid young man. There I learned the importance of being a good man, how to be a leader and how to treat all people with respect. During my time in the US Army and in Vietnam, I made a commitment to never have children outside of marriage. I thought of my mother often and truly missed my family. In December of 1968 I was discharged from the Army as a Sgt E-5 and a Bronze Star Recipient.

At 23 years old, I started night school at Nassau Community College in Garden City, New York, then transferred to Hofstra University. I graduated with a BBA in 1974. I had worked for the New York Telephone Company and Allstate Insurance Company while going to school. The 3M Company hired me that September, and I was transferred to Orange County, California in December of 1974.

I purchased my first house in Irvine, California in August of 1977. I recall telling my mother I bought a house in California for $71,000. She said, "Boy, you are rich now."

I replied, "Mother, it's a fixer-upper." But, I had come a long way from the one room in segregated, rural Tallahassee.

My mother was so proud of me when I got married on July 1, 1978 in Wilmington, Delaware. She was by my side when I said –I Do - to Audrey M Shockley, now my wife of 39 years. I was proud to have my mother by my side - because she made it possible for me, all my brothers and my sister!

Unfortunately, my mother passed away at the age of 57, as the mother of eight children. I always thought about how she had worked hard, and prayed hard, and dreamed, but never got her brick house.

In 1988, I purchased a new brick house in Atlanta, Georgia as tribute to my mother. That was a very special time for me and I knew she was watching me and my family grow. If she could have dropped in from Heaven, she would have smiled and been very proud of the brick house. She would have been prouder that my family and I are all Christians and we know and love the Lord!

In 1997, I was transferred to Ohio, and moved my wife and two daughters to West Chester from Atlanta. My real estate agent in Ohio called for details on the type of house, community and price range we were looking for. I told the agent, I wanted a *brick house,* in a community with sidewalks and excellent school system.

On our first visit to Ohio, the realtor showed us 8 houses and not one was a brick house. Now, as a salesman, I had been trained to focus on the customer. During our first phone conversation, I had told her I wanted a brick house! If she had just asked me "why" a brick house I could have shared that a brick house had been my mother's dream, and my mother's dream was now my dream. If only my real estate agent, had asked me "why" a brick house!

I would often say to my daughters, "Why do you think I wanted a brick house? Because my mother dreamed of a brick house." I wanted them to understand what my mother had meant to me growing up, and the brick house was a tribute to her.

In 2001, I took early retirement from 3M after 27 years as a Sales Representative and 8 years as an Account Executive. I retired in a position held by less than 5% of 3M Representatives - the best of the best!

I am blessed with two daughters. Shawna is married and a doctor at Johns Hopkins Medical Center in Maryland. We have one 2-year-old grandson and another due in December (2017). Our daughter Phylicia is a Gymnastic Coach in Ft. Mill, South Carolina. She is still looking for Mr. Right.

Eventually, we sold the brick house in Ohio and move to Raleigh, North Carolina where we live now. My wife and I discussed buying a brick house for North Carolina and settled on a stone & masonry house.

My life is my tribute to my mother.

* * * * *

The Least of These

Mark Heilshorn

The year was 1988. I had been working for the AmeriCares Foundation for two years. AmeriCares is a medical relief organization founded in 1979. Its primary purpose is to procure donated medicines and medical supplies needed to save lives around the world. As a Project Director, my role was to call on would-be donors and ask for medicines that could be used in a world of need. The goal was to find medicines with enough shelf life left to be distributed to doctors and clinics all around the world.

Usually a drug could not be sold with less than a two-year shelf life, and would otherwise be destroyed. By donating their excess supplies, companies could receive one and a half times what it cost to produce the drug. AmeriCares was one of a few organizations with the ability to take those donations and deliver them to victims of earthquake, volcano, tsunami, civil war hurricanes, floods, etc. Consider the opportunity for a company to cut its losses, donate products for a sizable write off, and save lives in distant lands that might be viable markets in the future. That was the goal at AmeriCares. Find those donations, identify the need around the world, be on the ground with reliable infrastructure to distribute the medicines and supplies, and provide life-saving products to people in need.

By 1988, I had traveled to serve the needy and poor in El Salvador, Haiti, Poland, the Philippines, and Lebanon. I remember thinking my job was the most exciting and powerful experience ever designed. None of my college peers could fathom the kinds of experiences and impact I was making. When describing an airlift taken to Cyprus to aid the beleaguered in Lebanon following the blockade of Beirut, I might as well have been talking about stories from Aesop's Fables. My life at that time was a labor of love; I saw my work as a ministry, and the experiences I would have would deeply impact my life and still does.

The impact AmeriCares had was largely influenced by its founder and maverick Bob Macauley. He thought nothing of contacting friends, and friends of friends, who served on the many Boards of these public companies to ask for the impossible. He would beg often on behalf of the many impoverished and suffering in the world. As relief agencies go, AmeriCares is one of the best. We were often first or close to first on the scene of a tragedy or natural disaster, out of pure grit and determination.

As a rule of thumb, not every disaster is natural. More often than not, tragedies are the result of a thousand bad decisions that lead to indifference, carnage and human suffering. In 1988, just such a disaster was thoroughly in the making in the Sudan and it would lead me to a life changing encounter.

The Sudan was in the middle of a massive civil war that year. Millions of Sudanese were being displaced. Men, women, and children were caught between the north led by the government of Khartoum, and the rebels of the south called the Sudanese Peoples Liberation Army (SPLA). This was a proxy battle between cold war foes Russia and the Unites States. Russia supported the dictatorship of the Khartoum government. America supported the democratic leader of the SPLA named John Gerang. Caught in the middle between warring factions were millions of lives.

In 1988 the world finally paid attention. Relief was in full swing. Concerts were planned; popular artists sang songs. Money was raised to send food, water, and medicines to the beleaguered, but very little ever left the docks in the port of Sudan. Nobody was strong enough to influence the tyrannical powers to serve the most in need. Taking a convoy of supplies into the bush was tantamount to death. I remember seeing footage of containers of food and supplies being dumped into the ocean to never see the light the day, and sadly never help those for which it was intended.

I'll never forget the day in September of 1988 when Bob Macauley asked me to come into his office. In my two years with AmeriCares, I had traveled extensively and seen the organization at work. But it still took my breath away when Bob innocently said, "Mark, we want you to go to Rome and encourage Mother Teresa to broker a cease fire in the Sudan so we can bring aid into the country."

I remember thinking this was a bad joke. Macauley was often quick with a lyric, joke or story. It was a mark of his brilliance and charm. It made him an extraordinary salesman, and an intensely powerful man who was loved and admired by many. But he was serious. I was shocked by the privilege of being asked to visit with one of the most revered people in the world. My mission was simple. Find Mother Teresa in Rome, deliver letters from Bob asking her to participate on our behalf, and negotiate when and where she could deliver.

I was 23, spoke no Italian, and was asked to negotiate with a world leader in a crisis nobody was able to solve. Brilliant!

Off to JFK I went with the bare essentials. A back pack, a package of letters, my passport and a stream of telexes telling me where in Rome I might find Mother Teresa. The trip to Rome was eventful. God has a funny sense of humor. There was a massive cold front whipping through the region that day, so the plane sat on the tarmac at JFK for at least three hours before we were able to lift off. The whole way to London I listened to a veteran of the Seven-Day War in Israel who talked the whole way about his tank battle, the Egyptians and battle still being waged in that region. It would prove to be a thoughtful beginning. The only time he stopped to listen to me was when I told him about my mission to meet Mother Teresa. I will never forget his words. He said, "She is a worker of miracles, go with God."

That was all the motivation I needed to keep going.

I arrived in Rome the next day after many layovers, flight changes and time changes. It was early afternoon. Once again,

I was simply following a spiritual guide. I didn't have many tools. Nobody was at the airport to greet me. There were no cell phones. Computers were a novelty. It was the land of gut instinct and a lot of risk. I remember simply going to the curb and hailing a taxi. One arrived and the driver lowered the passenger window. I simply said, "Mother Teresa."

To this day, I can still remember his eyes getting large and his hand gesturing to come into the taxi. He rambled with Italian, and tried to communicate with slow English. He could have taken me anywhere and I remember being very nervous – I had no idea where we were going. Slowly, he meandered through the nooks and crannies of Rome – we wandered down cobblestone streets that had no name, narrow as bike paths, strewn with gay couples, businessmen, and travelers enjoying the day. He stopped at a set of stairs and motioned up. All I could see were stairs, but I was told her Sisters of Charity home was at the top of the many stairs. I paid the driver in American dollars, grabbed my belongings and ascended.

Rome, as some of you know, is all stairs. After what seemed to be nine flights of stairs, I arrived, rang a doorbell and was welcomed. Thankfully I was expected. After such a long trip, I was eager to meet with Mother Teresa, explain my reason for being there, address the goals, set up the time frame for her involvement, get to my hotel, rest and report back to AmeriCares that the package had been delivered and mission accomplished. Instead, I was asked to wait until Mother Teresa was ready to receive me. I thought it would be an hour or so.

One hour went by, and I was told it would be a while more. Since she was not appearing, I decided to investigate my surroundings and perhaps pray with the other sisters who were dutifully preparing for their rounds in the city. As a spiritual man, I thought their practices would resonate with me. The sanctuary I entered was a renovated chicken coup. Where the hens used to lay their eggs was now an alter with candles and a cross. I started to pray with the sisters and quickly realized these faithful were praying way beyond my pithy practice. As it turns out, praying the rosary in their world meant praying for as long as a votive candle would burn. I found out later that they prayed on their knees for four hours before they went to serve the poor in Rome throughout the night.

It was about the forth hour of waiting that I finally saw Mother Teresa. Mind you, I was warned not to bow to her. At the time of the instruction, I wondered why I would ever bow or kneel. I was not Catholic, nor did I really understand the gesture. It was dark by now. The courtyard was empty and there she was. Mother Teresa was very short. No more than four feet six maybe. I was stunned by her stature, but what took my breath away was the halo above her head.

I had seen pictures of halo's, viewed portraits of angels and Jesus with halo's, but never imagined I would see an actual halo. There she was, and the halo was beaming bright. It took all my energy not to begin to kneel. She was graceful, light as a feather, warm and gentle but intense. She took my hands and prevented me from kneeling down. Instead she lifted me up and said, "We have been expecting you. How can I help?"

I found out later that she too, had been praying for four hours before meeting with me. Upon hearing that I had arrived, she kneeled and prayed. It was only when the flame had extinguished was she ready to speak to me.

What followed was a series of meetings over that weekend. She was not able to give me what I wanted – a commitment, a time frame, an answer. I flew back to AmeriCares without certainty. What she did give me was a profound sense that God was working wonders through people like her. Mother Teresa was a simple woman who had a simple dream to serve the poor and needy. One 'sister of charity' in Calcutta became a thousand in her lifetime. A small, delicate, graceful woman had more power and ability than a dozen heads of state.

108

The drive to save the Sudan was frustrating. It took about six months, but Mother Teresa did manage to intervene and forge a ceasefire. It lasted all of 48 hours. Long enough to bring some badly needed supplies to the interior of the country, but sadly, not enough time to do more good. As soon as the door opened, it closed, and to this day the Sudan is plagued by civil strife and famine. The carnage of this civil war still rages on.

As for me, my life was never the same. I realized that one life can make a big difference. I knew I was destined for more, and more had to be done. It would not be long after that I would apply to Yale Divinity School to study theology and become a pastor myself.

Mother Teresa was a bright, shining example of determination and stewardship. She left her mark on me in ways I am only now beginning to understand. To her tribute, she asked that nobody kneel to her because she felt everyone should be doing what she was. She was no better than others, just a far more faithful servant than most. That was her calling, and she felt everyone had the responsibility to share love and care for the 'least of these...' That is wealth on a level I can only hope to scratch. But, it is my goal to find a way to empower and lift up those in need and do my best to bind this world with God's grace and love.

Tough Love

Linda Strother

So, what does manifesting an abundance in health look like? It's not as tangible as perhaps manifesting a house, car or money; this is where the hard work comes in. The question is, what does it feel like to be in perfect health? I thought I had been in pretty good health most of my life; my genetics contributed to some of my good health over the years, but as we know, bad habits can catch up with us.

The phrase, "a picture of health" stirs up different images for everyone. What is your picture of health? For me it was fitting into a smaller size, getting my Type 2 Diabetes under control, but most of all feeling fit enough to work in my garden and travel.

The main catalyst for this particular journey was my daughter, a Registered Nurse. She treated me to a lovely holiday at the beach to celebrate my retirement. When we arrived, she planned to do some food shopping and asked what I wanted. I requested some snack foods and my favorite ice cream. Later that evening after a wonderful walk along the Carolina beach at sunset she said, "I want to talk to you seriously about something."

She started the conversation with, "You know I love you and will always take care of you when you are older, but wouldn't it be nice if you were healthier and could live a lot longer independently?"

What I heard her say was, "I don't care if you are fat, but it would be nice if you cared more for yourself."

Her words shocked me, as I was the person who had taught her about healthy eating. It was a bit embarrassing to find I was no longer the example for her on how to live a healthy life. I had let the stress of my job cause me to revert to poor eating habits. And really, I was only kidding myself that I was eating healthy. While it was true that my diet consisted of organic food, even organic ice cream is loaded with fat and carbohydrates, as were the potato chips I was so fond of.

I was not obese, but was 30 pounds overweight and my general health was spiraling downward. My daughter also mentioned that my A1C reports were 7.2 and my cholesterol was in the mid-200 range. Those are not good numbers for a diabetic to have.

Her care and concern spurred me into wanting to regain my health, but the question was; how to achieve this? I needed to do some deep thinking and meditation to understand what being healthy should look like now that I was in my sixties. I knew how it felt when I was younger but how it would look and feel once I accomplished my goal?

The physical process of losing weight is no secret; fewer calories in equals weight loss, and increased exercise raises the heart rate to burn fat. I understood that, but I had to look at my emotional reasons for not caring for my own health.

Over the years, I had gained and lost weight many times. I tried to eat healthy and organic, and was a vegetarian for many years. I spent the better part of 1991 eating a live-food-only diet but many years after that, I did not pay much attention to my health. Through it all, I had not been truly honest with myself. It's called being in denial.

When I was 12 years old, I had a mysterious disease that caused painful swelling of my joints. Doctors could not find the cause until my mother took me to an Osteopath. He told her to take me off white sugar, white flour, sodas, and highly salted and fatty foods like bacon and potato chips. After a few weeks, the swelling abated. Of course, as a teenager I reverted to terrible food and life choices as well. But then, at 18, I became a vegetarian and learned to meditate and practice yoga. At 19, I could do a handstand and I felt my mind and body were aligned.

That same year I fell in love, married and again fell into poor health habits. I gained 180 pounds in less than 3 years and once again suffered from painful joints. In addition, I had terrible stomach problems, migraines and an overall feeling of sadness. A year after the birth of my son, I decided to gain control of my life again. I began to eat well, followed a vegetarian lifestyle and practiced yoga daily.

Like many people, I had tried many diets over the past 50 years; Weight Watchers, Vegan, the Grapefruit Diet, Adkins, Low-Carb, Raw Foods. etc. I have tried them all and they all worked, for a while. Again, like many people, the reason they never worked very long for me is I was not addressing the source of my dis-ease with myself.

During some meditation and quiet reflection, I finally got to the root of my problem; when I was a kid we were not allowed sugary foods and it was a rare treat to have ice cream or sweets. I also used sweets as a reward with my own kids, calling snack foods "treats." But it was not until I was on a beach holiday that I truly understood the effect this had on my health. We had eaten very well the entire vacation, but one afternoon someone in our group said, "Let's find an ice cream parlor, we deserve a treat."

It was like one of those light bulb moments, and I realized why I craved sweets and treats. Deep down, I associated the sugary foods with approval. I found that an emotional response to something negative triggered the need to feel good about myself, so I would have a "treat." Ice Cream, candy, and potato chips, are my go-to foods when stress triggers negative reactions. The realization of it hit me so strongly, I could not finish my ice cream cone and actually threw it in the bin.

As we know, too much of this food causes disease and obesity. I would eat to feel better, but then the cycle began all over again when I looked in the mirror or tried on clothes. One of the worst experiences was trying on clothes in department store dressing rooms. The stark bright lights bring all your flaws into focus.

Mindset plays an important role in obtaining good health and maintaining your healthy goals. It's no secret that negative thoughts and feelings can manifest into the physical body. Find the mental picture in your mind's eye of you in perfect health, perfect weight or whatever your desire in health may be. For me it was a picture in my mind of the pure joy of childhood, running playing and laughing with no limitations. I had a vision in my mind of what I wanted to look like and what I wanted my blood sugar reports to read. I did a lot of self-talk too. Asking myself: *Do I really need a second helping of that very yummy meal?* I would say: *No you do not need a second helping, walk it off, and distract yourself.*

It is not always a smooth journey to a healthy life. There are always bumps along the way. Today, I have found a balance in my life but there are days when I lose control, especially during the holidays or under great stress.

The very day I reached my weight goal, I celebrated with a cream filled chocolate éclair. I noticed, as I was halfway through consuming the pastry, that it tasted greasy and fatty. It was then that I said out loud to myself to "Stop eating the pastry."

The cost of that pastry added up to 400 calories and 80 carbs. There is no point in getting angry with yourself. You just need to move on, accept that you may have some weak moments and get back on track.

After losing weight I did not have any clothes that fit, so I had to face the dreaded department store dressing room mirrors again. But this time what I found was I had dropped three sizes in jeans. I was amazed and re-checked the sizes several times to make sure they were not sized incorrectly. For a new "treat" I purchased several pairs of jeans and bought some new earrings.

Although it was hard to hear at the time, I appreciate my daughter speaking up. Before I started this journey, I went to my doctor for testing and advice. She was very supportive. With her approval, I chose to consume 1200 net calories a day. In 2014, I lost a total of 35 pounds and brought my blood sugar readings down to below diabetic standards. It took me 9 months to lose the weight correctly.

I used one of the many fitness applications that you can find on your smart phone, computer or tablet. The app helped monitor what I ate and tracked my exercise. I also synced it with an activity bracelet to help monitor my day. Fitness apps are a great way to keep track of your day, however you must be perfectly honest with yourself. Record everything you eat and drink, and count every step and every bit of exercise too. You will be amazed at how much you really eat and how quickly the exercise adds up. I used to think that I did not consume all that many calories in a day, but I was fooling myself.

It's now almost four years later; I am working a very physical job, I have not had a cold, flu or allergies or even a hint of illness for four years.

I am too busy to allow illness to enter my mind or my life. Abundance of health is my personal goal, to feel truly great physically and mentally. For me it means feeling great when I wake up to be able to work a physical job at 63 years old as well as garden and travel. I still keep track of my fitness goals by using my activity bracelet to measure how many steps I take daily. I also find if I don't count my calories and enter them into the fitness application, I tend to eat more.

Manifesting abundance in all areas of your life is a journey; think of it as building muscle. When you build muscle and are physically fit, your body holds the memory of that perfection. It's like muscle memory; at some point in your life you have established what is perfect health for you. Your body and mind remembers even if we get bogged down with stress or negative thoughts. It just takes a moment to recall the good feeling and you are back on track. As my brilliant Aussie friend Isabella would say, "You need to have a mindset for success."

I am dedicated to maintaining my abundance of health. Not only by using my mental exercises but by making healthy choices every day.

There are times when I fall off my path, but I have the choice everyday to choose better health. Recently I suffered a death in my family, a health scare for myself and purchased a new house. I must be honest, I did fall off my path a bit during these intensely stressful times but it was easy to step back on the right track.

Abundance in health is obtainable, it really is.

I wish you abundance in all aspects of your life.

I Never Got on the Plane

Neville Gaunt

Ordinarily, when someone has been in corporate life since leaving university, the next job is likely to be more of the same. And that was my thinking when I was in the final throws of handing over my many roles to the new company that had purchased my employer in 2001 for £3bn in a corporate takeover. Even the exit package I received that provided for career mentoring had reinforced the expectation that I would follow the same corporate path. "The King is dead, long live the King!" After all, I had a lot of experience that was in high demand in a market with limited supply.

I had a few offers to consider, and going straight back into a senior and stressful role heading up the financial team of an oil company seemed to be my destiny. But, it also felt like a form of entrapment. My roles in the last three years had given me a lot of responsibility, independence, and job satisfaction; and I couldn't see that would be repeatable somewhere else. I already knew this new company was unwilling to allow me to fill multiple roles, as they were about to split them up across their group. I loved a lot of my job and put up with the business-as-usual and politics because I felt valued and knew I was making a difference. However much I may have wanted to jump ship and start afresh, I felt trapped. I did not believe I was cut-out to do anything else; I had just turned 41 years old, was corporate and internationally experienced, and all the advice pointed me down one route. How wrong that thought was!

It all started to change when...

It was a just normal Sunday; I played dad-taxi and watched the boys play football in the morning, came home to a Sunday family lunch, with everyone sitting together listening to the plans for the week ahead. With 2 teenagers and 3 at junior school, the conversation was, let's say, random! It was a time for me to do my dad bit as the next two weeks I would be in another country. There was nothing unusual in that, as my job involved lots of travelling.

It was late, and long after the kids had gone to bed that I received a fax saying:

"I know it's late but give me a call when you get this. Cheers, Rusty"

An innocuous fax followed by a short call later was nothing special or unusual, but it started a chain of events that would be a defining moment in my future. The phone call was a brief discussion about changing my meeting schedule. The meetings scheduled at the beginning of my trip would now be held at the end because the golf course drawings weren't ready. The golf course we were planning at the time is today known as Liberty National Golf Course. The project Rusty and I had managed together for nearly 10 years had changed the fortune of a parcel of heavily contaminated land, from a liability of over $100 million to an asset of over $30 million.

The upshot of the fax and phone call meant I had two days in the London office and now would just travel on Wednesday. Plans changing were a common event in my life - my diary was never what you might call fixed!

So, Wednesday 12 September 2001 was the day I was now scheduled to fly to the USA to finalise the handover of my employer's USA operations to the new corporate team based in Houston. But as you may recall, the events of the day before changed the world.

There wasn't a plane to be seen in the sky on Wednesday 12 September 2001, as flights were grounded all over the globe. I never even made it to the airport because the day before was

9/11/2001 or simply just 9/11, a day all the world will remember. As the cliché goes, it was the first day of the rest of my life.

Changing times

Prior to that fateful day, my successful and stressful career had mostly been in the oil and gas industry, and before that came cement manufacture and construction. I was lucky that I had been exposed to all sorts of opportunities; from learning what made the business tick, and its commercial foundations; to financing and restructuring; mergers and acquisition; and starting new business ventures, and exiting others. I also had bosses that were great leaders, although in my early career I didn't really know what leadership was, as it wasn't a term frequently used as it is today. As I now know far more about what leadership means, I know they were great leaders and they had one thing in common - they believed in me. I was hungry to learn and do new things and they would always give me the chance to do them. I may not have said thank you enough at the time, but I am grateful to all of them!

So, in the aftermath of the 9/11 disaster, at the ripe old age of 41, I started to think differently and they were pretty radical thoughts even for me.

What if I did not do what everyone else did, and thought I should do?

What if I declined their invitation to rejoin the rat-race?

Am I screwing up a career?

Am I being selfish?

What makes me believe I can do things others have tried and failed to do?

Am I nuts to even entertain these ideas?

I know my party-piece at Christmas was singing "My Way", but come on Neville get a grip!

I was lucky as I had Nicola, a smart and very supportive wife. Nicola is my second wife, and at the time we'd been married 4 months. Before 9/11, she and I both expected me to slip into a new corporate role. Imagine what her thoughts were when I dropped this bombshell on her! The questions going through my mind would be simpler to answer for an 18-year-old with no ties, but for a married-with-children 41-year-old with our lifestyle?

Did I have the courage to do it?

What did I want to do?

Could it support our lifestyle?

What about a lifestyle change?

Will our savings support us long enough?

Where is this taking us?

I knew I could not change things overnight, as I had a wife and family to support; but my new path was set in motion, even though I had no idea what twists and turns that path might have. And believe me there have been many, too many to list here! But they all had a common theme – they challenged the status quo. Although I operated with a "if it ain't bust, don't fix it" mentality, I couldn't abide living in a job that needed a business-as-usual attitude. Even as a child, I was always looking to do things better, and that sometimes meant starting from scratch. I was also fascinated by the internet and loved turning data into decision-making. New concepts, products and service ideas could help people improve as the dot.com explosion broke the communication barriers. My transferable skills had all been put to good use – even a somewhat useless MBA in marketing came into play!

119

Go out there and change the world

I decided not to fall into another corporate role, and took a few consultancy projects where I had far more control of my time. But moving from being salaried to being a consultant was a far bigger adjustment than I expected. It had many challenges, not least was the absence of the monthly pay cheque! But, it's amazing what you can do when you have to. It's vitally important to have a supportive partner who's with you all the way in the new programme! The kids were still growing up, and fortunately we didn't put their lives on hold - they now had the added benefit of seeing even more of me. Although my nagging them to do homework might not be a benefit in their eyes!

Apart from consultancy work and helping startups, I survived by sharing my experiences, too. I have done my fair share of keynote and public speaking over the years. I was lucky to not only have plenty of practical on-the-job experiences of leadership and teamwork, but the training courses were second to none. One crisis management course I recall required me to escape from an upturned helicopter in water and in pitch black conditions – which in itself needs little training as survival is an inbuilt mechanism in the human body! You might ask why an accountant would ever be in that situation, but it was all about leadership and crisis management. It also makes for an interesting after dinner speech!

About 8 years into that journey, I stumbled into a networking event with a keynote speaker talking about people and improving performance. I say stumbled because it was more by accident I was there, as I was a last-minute substitute and going as a favour to a friend. I went rather reluctantly, as over the years I have heard many inspirational speakers, had multiple months of leadership training, done the Tony

Robbins fire-walk twice(!), bought the T-Shirt, etc. I wasn't expecting a great deal of anything new.

This speaker was a gentleman named Graham Williams. In 45 minutes, he proved to me that, within reason, I could do and have whatever I really wanted. Now, you may have already had an experience where you found a way to get something that you really wanted. I'd always believed that was possible, and I had done it regularly, but this guy was talking about something radically different. Because this was a scientific approach - and like a chemistry experiment that gives the same results every time - it was a process that guaranteed success. The light bulbs in my mind were like a firework show that I did not want to end.

He had a simple message;

"What I did and how I did it has a science behind it."

The next time I saw Graham, it was on a Saturday morning, along with what were intended to be partners in a new venture. I knew someone was joining the meeting to present his approach, but didn't connect the dots that this was the same guy – I'd not even been told his name. So, when Graham turned up I was interested! More light bulbs shone brightly as Graham presented. As he and I talked and challenged each other, it was as though we'd jumped onto a lift going to the 50th floor leaving the others standing in the lobby. It was pretty clear we were on a different planet, and very soon after that we created Mind Fit Ltd.

What I have subsequently learned, and we have proven in the last 8 years, is that you can actually apply this science to anything you do, and be the best you can be. The only provision to that is, you must have a deep inner purpose, want it, and be prepared to change to achieve it. That change will likely be a shift in your beliefs and attitude.

This new path I chose some 16 years ago has brought me to something very special. The irony is that the information has been known at least since 1892:

"The greatest discovery of our generation is that human beings, by changing the inner attitudes of their mind, can change the outer aspects of their lives."
   ~ 1892, William James, the Father of Modern Psychology

If you want a quote that is more commonly known and my favorite:

"If you think you can do a thing or think you can't do a thing, you're right."

~ Henry Ford

This Ford quote I have liked for nearly 30 years, and now I get it!

Now the real challenge

Before I met Graham, I was looking for something to make a big change. Believing I had found it, I now had to prove it would work in the most difficult and complex of situations. Otherwise, it would be just another shiny object that only works for a few. In this particular case, it could turn out to be the newest flash-in-the-pan leadership program that only occasionally worked under very specific conditions. So, over the past few years Graham and I built a small team and have proven the science over and over again in all sorts of contexts. We have proven it in enough arenas to be able to do the unthinkable in people and organisational change programmes – we guarantee it!

Inherently, we all know that the right positive mental attitude and a will to succeed are ingredients that are vital to improvement and success. So, when you do hit that impasse, that brick wall, it will not stop you. And yes, brick walls are everywhere and you'll hit them; but this time you will have the ability to scale it, go round it, over it or knock it down to continue your path. I believed we had found the missing link so anyone could really succeed.

We're still aiming to prove it everywhere, and we're a long way along the road in doing it so the journey continues.

Globally connected

As we know the world is changing. Travel and the internet have made it a far smaller, more accessible planet than at any time in history. That opens up many more opportunities than I could have dreamed of as a child, a baby-boomer born in 1959. To take advantage of the opportunities, we have to be personally ready to see them; and have the confidence, courage and commitment to then choose to take them. We need to build relationships and collaborate not just locally but globally, and in person as well as in the digital world.

Can we guarantee we are all ready to do it?

I ask leaders and managers of all organisations, "Do people go to work to fail?"

Who would answer: "Yes!"?

So why is it we don't help people succeed and be happier?

Why not help them be the best they can be?

Won't that make them more engaged in what they do and happier too?

What I learned in 2001 was that I really had a choice. I had a dream to go and change the world. I had no idea at the time how I was going to do it. I stumbled across something that will help anyone be better if they want to be better.

So, if you believe you have a choice - what's yours?

A Player's Coach

Andy Olds

I am one of seven kids. I grew up in a very small farming town, and if pressed, I would say we were economically poor people. But when I was young, money was not something I really noticed and no one ever talked about it. I can't remember feeling like we lacked anything. I do remember people dropping off clothes to my house in paper sacks. I can remember going to the store right across the street to get more milk. We had such a large family, we would use three to four gallons of milk a day. I also remember my mom paying the grocery bill once a month; which was between $300-$450. That was back in the 1970's.

As a kid, I loved to be outdoors. I was fairly athletic, excelled in baseball & football, and even played a little bit of basketball. Following three older brothers and two sisters through a small town high school, everyone knew me as "one of the Olds kids". Fortunately, the last name of Olds had a fairly good reputation.

I was very close to my mom & dad. I know they loved us; they set rules and expectations, took care of our needs, and raised us to be responsible people. The 1960's and 70's were not an era where people said they loved you or gave you a kiss at night – I just wasn't raised that way. Although that didn't happen, I still knew without a shadow of a doubt that my parents loved me very, very much.

So, my basic needs were met and I had plenty of siblings, activities, parental love and folks looking out for me. What I did lack though, was a great deal of confidence. Whether it was in math class or sports, I lacked confidence in myself. I just didn't let people know it.

When I graduated high school, I thought I should go to college, but my ACT score was very bad. I hadn't earned the greatest grades, either. I had an older brother go to West Point. He was my big brother, my idol, and I wanted to follow in his footsteps and go to West Point. But because my test scores were so poor, my only option was to go to preparatory school at Fort Dix in New Jersey. By the time I got my paperwork in to register for Fort Dix, I was number 501; the first alternate. I had to wait until the middle of August to see if at least one of those first 500 applicants would opt out, or get hurt, or get cold feet. But all 500 cadets accepted their nominations and went to preparatory school. So, I spent that year working in a factory.

My mom had arranged this job for me. I traveled about 40 minutes a day by car, and worked for minimum wage; $3.15 an hour. Eventually I would get fired from this job. By this time, I knew that I wanted to go to college so I applied to Capital University in Columbus, Ohio. Again, my poor grade point average (GPA) and ACT score haunted me. The only way Capital would accept me was after I completed a 6-week summer program called Foundations. This program was for applicants who had low ACT scores and bad GPAs. I took English and Speech classes for an hour and a half every day for 6 weeks. There were 32 people in the class when we started, and we ended with 26. I finished first in my class in Speech, and second in English. I was excited to finish that way; it did a lot for my confidence. I had just confirmed that I was smarter than my grades demonstrated, but that also meant I was responsible for the poor ACT scores and bad grades.

At Capital University, I had a pretty good college career. Like a lot of people, my first semester was a struggle, but once I got into the classes specific to my major, I made the Dean's List four semesters in a row. I was also a 4-year letterman at football. The defensive coordinator of the football team was also the head baseball coach. He knew that I had a love for baseball as well, and wanted me to play. But I told him I just wasn't a good enough athlete to play baseball and football; I'd just end up being terrible at both. So, he let me coach baseball when I wasn't playing football. I learned a lot about baseball from him.

The Thursday prior to our season opener in football at Capital, we were having walk-throughs. For some reason, I looked over my shoulder. And to my great surprise, I saw my brother Steve. At first, I thought: *Awesome, Steve has driven almost 2 hours to watch me practice.*

And then reality sunk in. He had made the drive to Columbus to tell me that our mom had suddenly and unexpectedly died that morning from a massive heart attack. She was 48 and I was 19. That event changed my life. I realized that my lack of a real, mature relationship with Mom was something I didn't wanted to repeat.

Three years later, I would lose my dad to cancer. He was 53. Dad was able to fight it for about 11 months. I did everything possible in those 11 months to get to know him and to develop a relationship that I would cherish my entire life.

Two years after I graduated, I was teaching at a small country school when I was offered an opportunity to be a graduate assistant at Indiana University and coach baseball for them. While I coached baseball, they would pay for me to get my Master's Degree. However, the graduate assistant position had been promised to someone who had played baseball at Indiana so they had first right of refusal. Once again, I found myself on the outside looking in. But because the coach wanted me badly enough, they secured a teaching assistant position for me instead. That meant just two years out of college myself, I was teaching classes in the sports science program at Indiana University and coaching baseball. Remember, I'm the guy that struggled with confidence. I found myself coaching players like Mickey Morandini, who played on an Olympic team and went on to play for the Cubs, and John Wehner of the Pittsburgh Pirates. I was surrounded with phenomenal athletes and found it a little overwhelming; since I didn't have much confidence in myself. I enjoyed coaching, however, because I had an opportunity to meet new people and to sharpen my craft.

After that year, I was invited to stay on at Indiana and coach baseball full time. I decided to turn them down, get married and go back to teaching at the small country high school. They had given me a year's leave of absence to get my Master's, so I returned. I coached football for them for six seasons, as an assistant coach and eventually defensive coordinator. In that time, I had multiple opportunities to become the head coach; I was offered the job, and turned it down behind closed doors simply because I felt like I wasn't qualified. I felt like even after playing football in college, I didn't know enough about the game. I didn't think I was smart enough to be head coach; all the other head coaches that I knew were much smarter than me. The one thing that I knew that I was good at, my strength, was building relationships with players. Sometimes in coaching, people try to categorize you; Are you a tactician? Are you a coach's coach? Are you a player's coach? Well, I clearly knew who I was; I was a player's coach. I felt that I could get my kids to play harder and better for me because we had a connection. We had a relationship.

After six years at this high school, not only was I an assistant football coach, but I was also the head baseball coach. I walked away from that for an opportunity to be a full-time assistant football coach at a bigger and more well-known school in Cincinnati. I eventually became the defensive coordinator at

Kings High School and I was really enjoying it. By my thirteenth season of coaching high school football I had turned down head coaching opportunities at least four times. People had called and asked me to come in and interview to take a job, and I turned them down every single time. My goal wasn't to be a head football coach; my goal was just to be a coach. I was going to be a worker bee and to do the things behind the scenes. I just never felt like I was called to be a head football coach, never once in my entire life.

But that year, amidst some strange circumstances within our football team, our head football coach resigned almost immediately after our season ended. There were a lot of sad players the day he resigned; it's a very sad time when a coach resigns quickly and urgently as he did. I sat in the back of the auditorium, kind of in shock myself and saddened, knowing how the kids felt as he made the announcement. Once the players were dismissed, they immediately circled me and told me I was going to be the next head football coach at Kings. They gave me their total support.

"Coach Olds," they told me, "You're the guy...you're the one to lead us...you're the next coach at Kings... we want you."

Well, as I smiled and thanked them, inside I was humbled, overwhelmed, and really, really scared. I thought: *These guys have no idea that I have zero confidence in myself, that I'm not smart enough to be a head football coach. They don't know I've turned down four other jobs before now.*

After the announcement in the auditorium, I spent the next day or two in shock. Then the athletic director approached me and said, "Andy would you be interested in interviewing for the head football job?"

"Well, I'm not sure," I answered. "I want a chance to talk to my pastor at my church, and more importantly, I want to talk to my wife."

When I got home and talked to my wife about it, she was so excited for me it made me scared. She obviously didn't see the lack of confidence that I had in myself. Evidently, she saw something in me that I didn't see, that I couldn't see – and that was I could be a successful coach. After a lot of prayer, and a lot of meetings with my pastor, who is a great friend of mine, I decided to interview for that job.

Two more days went by, and the athletic director again said, "Hey Andy, are you going to interview for this job?"

And I said, "Yes, I am."

"Well, you have to apply for it first." We both laughed. I had never interviewed for an internal job like this before. I didn't know the process.

So, I applied for the job and the interview was that same night. Because I taught physical education, my dress wardrobe was limited to two ties and one suit. I had on my one suit, and I'm sure I looked like I felt - quite uncomfortable. I interviewed with seven different people all at the same time. I've referred to it as 'The Spanish Inquisition.' They fired all sorts of questions at me for two hours and fifteen minutes. But in those two hours and fifteen minutes of questions, no one asked me how we were going to win games. No one asked me to draw up a particular defense, or a specific scenario. Not one question was asked about what play would work best, what defense would work best, or how to evaluate talent. None of those football questions came up. But what they did ask me over the course of two hours and fifteen minutes were all kinds of questions about kids. About building relationships and kids. I was surprised. I still had no idea of the importance of relationships; that what they valued most in a head coach was what came naturally to me. I still wasn't sure I was the right guy for the job.

I was living in Wilmington at the time, which was about forty-five minutes from the school. When I got home at quarter to eleven that night, my wife was waiting up for me and she said, "You need to call the athletic director right now."

This was in 1997, we didn't have cell phones back then, at least I couldn't afford one. So, I called my athletic director back immediately, and he said, "Coach Olds, I want you to know we'd like to hire you as the next head football coach if you are willing to take the job."

Forty-two people had applied for this job, and I was the first person they interviewed. They didn't interview another soul and I took the job.

That first year was like a whirlwind. A lot of coaches build their staff with people who are great technical football minds. People who are up on the latest and greatest schemes. No one told me how to build a staff; I just built our staff on what I knew and how I felt. I hired the teachers that had the greatest relationships with the kids. It didn't matter how much football they knew, but they had to love kids and love education. We made a lot of mistakes in that first year, but ended the season 9-1, tied for the league championship. Here I am, this first-year head coach, a guy who had previously turned down four jobs because I didn't have the confidence to be a successful head coach, had the most important thing; I knew how to build relationships with kids. I'm still coaching today, I just finished my nineteenth season. In those nineteen seasons as a head coach, we've won the league championship twelve times and had thirteen playoff appearances.

Building relationships goes way beyond my players, I have great relationships with my coaches. Kings has the least amount of turnover in coaches that most schools in Southwest Ohio because I give my coaches a lot of latitude to make decisions. As head coach, I oversee twenty coaches and the whole program of about 250 kids. But on Friday nights, game nights, I'm just a simple assistant coach, coaching one position. We have a defensive coordinator, and offensive coordinator, and special teams coordinator, I let those people make decisions and practice plans, evaluate players, and make suggestions. They're invested. They've got an emotional investment in our program. It must be working because when you come to a Kings football game on any Friday night, you can see anywhere from fifteen to twenty-five former players on our sideline. I think that's really unique and we welcome those kids.

I have another relationship building opportunity when I'm not coaching football. I'm the national director for the NFL's Play60 character program. That allows me to travel from city to city talking about Play60's health and wellness messaging for youth. More importantly, we talk about character building, and how important it is to play and live your life with character. I have an opportunity to not only impact players and students, I have a greater opportunity to influence coaches. I get to be a character coach for twenty to thirty brand new coaches in every city I visit. The message that these coaches hear from me is the effect that they have on the kids and the right way to do it. These kids aren't really impressed with how many championships you've won or how many games you've won. They're more impressed and have more respect for you if you can remember their name, and you care what kind of day they've had at school, and you ask questions to check on their family. Those are the things that will connect you and help you build relationships with your players and students.

I can't completely explain all the success we've had in Kings football. I do believe that God finally painted me into a corner and said, "Andy Olds, it is time to be a head football coach. This is what you've been wired to do." – even before I knew it myself. I never had an inkling, never had the desire, never mentioned to anybody in my family or anybody I ever played with, "Someday I want to be a head football coach." I was the last guy in the room that would have ever answered the question, "Hey how many of you want to be head football coach?" You would have never seen my hand up.

* * * * *

Jennifer's Jewelry

Lisa Baird Panos

Not many women of my generation can boast a Lindsay Lohan portrayal in a major motion picture. To be clear, my non-existent twin and I never tried to reunite my parents and I've never had the pleasure of cosmically changing places with my mother.

But I *was* a Mean Girl.

The idyllic town near Columbus, Ohio, where I spent my formative years, and where I currently reside, is referred to as "The Bubble." Affectionately named for its ability to remain immune to issues plaguing the rest of the United States, "The Bubble" is both a blessing and a curse. My hometown isn't one of those newly chartered suburbs infested with McMansions and overrun with superficial conversations littered with false humility. No. Where I grew up, wealth wasn't flaunted, it was understood. Success wasn't a goal, it was a destiny. The only true strife that invaded "The Bubble" was when someone, whether an outsider or a rebellious child, thumbed his or her nose at these simple social contracts. There was no room for error.

And I might as well have been named Error.

In the third grade, I transferred from public school to a private, all-girls school because I clearly wasn't already insulated enough and needed a protective uniform skirt and knee-high socks. I settled in immediately, permanently nestled at the bottom of my class and was held back to repeat third grade. Over the next few years, my consistency was truly remarkable as I maintained my class rank of 52, grateful that no one else transferred in to push me down to 53.

That was about the only number I focused on, however, as my math grades remained quite low and when it came time to read out loud in English class, I tried to mimic my more well-adjusted classmates and quickly recite passages. Except when they did it, they sounded like Shakespeare actresses and I fumbled over my words and sounded more like one of Shakespeare's drunken fools. By this time, it wasn't even my success, or lack thereof, that concerned me. In my mind, I knew I was intelligent and had the nature and nurture necessary for achievement. It was the laughter from my classmates, the placating clichés from other parents and the exasperation of my own that left me feeling poor. Satisfaction should have been my wealth currency, but I was beginning to show signs of abject poverty.

As I entered middle school, I did what any self-conscious, but self-respecting pre-teen would do. I imprisoned my insecurity behind a wall, relying on bricks composed of malicious insults, deflecting rumors about my peers and faked ambivalence. If someone committed an unforgivable act like a misplaced chuckle in the classroom or a misinterpreted glance in the hallway, I would convene the Unicorn (my school mascot) UN and immediately begin building a coalition against the offending party.

Once, I singled out a classmate named Jennifer. I don't remember all of her crimes against humanity, but I do know that she wore a pair of Gloria Vanderbilt jeans that I found particularly offensive. I spent seconds branding a new secret society named the "I Hate Jennifer Club." Loyal members were required to wear a specific bracelet to show the world their collective displeasure for Ms. Vanderbilt's designs and Jennifer herself. If club members didn't follow MY rules, punishment was handled swiftly (by me of course) with further ridicule and public shaming.

One of my eye-opening moments was a party at a club member's house on an area river. It was the typical gathering of that age and at the time I was delighted by the fact that nearly all attendees were wearing our club bracelets. All except Jennifer, of course, who also attended the party. We gathered on the dock and while I don't recall the substance of those conversations, I do distinctly remember my graceful nosedive into the stagnant river and the hearty and cathartic laughter as I broke the surface.

I emerged from that river feeling like the Emperor with no clothes. Or at least thoroughly saturated ones. It occurred to me at that moment that none of my classmates actually liked me. They were frightened they would be the next name to grace my jewelry. It was a crushing realization, but while I was out of the water, I was into bullying way too deeply to take a healthy breath.

As if things weren't bad enough, my parents received a letter from my Headmaster that very same year. I won't bore you with the entire contents, but hearing your mother and father recite the following phrases will shake your own personal bubble to its foundation:

> *"One has to only meet Lisa and talk with her to know she is both bright and inquisitive...what then is missing? Quite frankly we don't know."*

> *"Whatever the reason, we are all hopeful the maturity she gains over the summer will enable her to recognize the disastrous effect that her present patterns have over her own academic development."*

> *"Lisa must face reality, and reality requires noticeable improvement in academic effort and achievement if Lisa is to continue at this school."*

So that happened. But it only caused me to double-down on my attacks against my wholly undeserving classmates. I didn't see any way out of the academic and social pit I had dug for myself other than to stand on the shoulders of my peers as I sought escape. But I am proud to say that it finally caught up with me. I was called into the principal's office for a particularly vicious verbal attack.

Sitting in that confined and suffocating space, I was forced to confront my latest victim and listen to her plainly list all of my shortcomings. I was mean. I was hateful. I was manipulative. Each description, while accurate, was a crushing blow and I couldn't wait to retaliate. But when the principal finally addressed me and asked why I had selected this particular person, I was stupefied. I couldn't think of one thing. Not. One. Thing.

While I wasn't blissfully ignorant of the rationale for my actions, in that moment it was inescapable that it was ME I didn't like. As with most bullies across generation, across region and across gender, I was misplacing my frustration and self-loathing. My three-day suspension was one of the most soul-baring and soul-saving periods of my life. While she refrained from crafting any bracelets, my mother basically gave me the 'Jennifer treatment' for the duration of my punishment. The only thing that made it worse was that I knew I deserved every second of it.

I thought the humiliation of being kicked out of school for three days would suffocate me. And of course when I returned to school, I was greeted by exactly what I deserved. For the first time, everyone was pointing at me and laughing with gleeful abandon. But surprisingly, I was actually *relieved and grateful* for my extended timeout. Exposing myself for who I was meant no more popularity contest, no more personal attacks. I could start over without worrying about social strata or seriously lacking self-esteem. I learned joy came from being honest, vulnerable and exposed. And that included loving myself, flaws and all. I didn't have to compare myself to anyone else. I could be me. And that was enough.

I would love to say I turned my life around on the spot. Unfortunately, our lives are rarely that easy. It took years of self-reflection and self-actualization to fully acknowledge my bullying tendencies. But I truly believe that despite my detours into the travel industry, higher education and non-profit fundraising, that suspension was the tipping point that dumped me into my true calling as a Life Coach. My atonement manifests itself in committing my life to empowering my clients, the readers of my first book *Big Girl Pants* and each and every audience I address.

I am still friends with the girls I bullied during my formative years. In fact, while I was writing this, I took a mental health break to call Jennifer. We laughed and reminisced and I professed my belated appreciation for her wardrobe. The unfortunate reality is that I'm not unique. Whether in an all-girls school in the 1970s, the offices of a Fortune 500 company or the streets of any city in the world, when we are feeling afraid, insecure and satisfaction-poor, our self-preservation tendencies channel our inner honey badger and we lash out with razor sharp claws in the direction of anyone unfortunate enough to be within striking distance.

This Darwinian reflex is powerful and pervasive, but what if we use our powers for good? What if we channel this energy into honest introspection and creating what our souls crave instead of ridiculing what we fear? What if we work toward developing authenticity in our professional lives and in our most critical personal relationships? What if we didn't chase arbitrary metrics of success and instead focused on meaningful, personal wealth like the satisfaction that I so desperately craved growing up? Answering these questions for myself has been my roadmap and my north star as I reinvented myself here in my fifth decade and as I continue my self-induced rehab from being a Mean Girl.

One of my favorite colloquialisms, which I will paraphrase to reflect my silver-screen self and bullying past, is: *"What Lindsay says about Jennifer says infinitely more about Lindsay than it does about Jennifer."*

I wonder if THAT would fit on a bracelet.

Superman in Disguise

Tyler Cerny

Most children would argue that summertime is the best time of the year. They are free at last from monotonous 7-hour school days. Time is only measured by the number of pickup basketball games, impromptu games of capture the flag and days spent at the swimming pool. As a child, however, my summertime days were measured in food. At seven years old, my breakfast alone consisted of 3 bowls of sugar-coated cereal, numerous powdered doughnuts and a box of Pop-tarts. My lunches and dinners were composed largely of fast food with routine trips to McDonald's where I consumed two double-cheeseburgers, two chicken sandwiches, French fries, a large strawberry milkshake and large root beer with endless refills.

These poor eating habits were the foundation of my struggle with obesity. Coupled with excessive amounts of television while my parents were working hard to make ends meet, my lifestyle was far from healthy. My lenient grandmother took care of my brother and I most days and unlike many grandmothers, mine did not show her love through warm, home-cooked meals. But since she was our primary caretaker, fast food, canned ravioli, and powdered doughnuts became my best friends. I was just a kid living and loving life, and I remained largely unaware that my eating habits could significantly affect my quality of life.

The teasing started in kindergarten where kids came up with cruel nicknames and jokes about my weight. One year on Halloween, my Superman costume was met with harsh jokes by the kids in my class who said that I was a fat Superman and too big to fly. I was also routinely referred to as "fat cheese".

Degrading remarks were directed at me all through my elementary school years.

At the time, I coped with the teasing by laughing along and joking with the other kids. I often deflected by coming up with jokes of my own about other kids to take the attention away from myself. To be honest, at this point, it appeared that I embraced my weight and never took the jokes personally. However, subconsciously, it greatly affected my self-confidence. My dreams and aspirations were limited and defined by my weight.

In my second-grade class, we were visited by a Cleveland Policeman who gave a presentation and showed all the students his patrol car. I was inspired by the policeman's words and felt a great affinity to the job's emphasis on protecting the community. Weeks later, I was asked in an assignment to write down what I wanted to be when I grew up. I immediately thought of the policeman and how I, too, wanted to help and protect my family and friends. In my best handwriting, I wrote down policeman. But, there was one word missing. I could never be just a policeman. I could only be a fat one. I felt that I could never escape my identity as overweight and obese.

When I was 9 years old, I stepped on the scale and saw the number 165.7 blinking back at me. I cautiously asked my friends at school how much they weighed, and all their responses were under 110 pounds. All those jokes and nicknames came rushing back to me and I felt the full pain of the insults. I saw that everyone else viewed my weight as a direct reflection of the person I was. This was the first time I truly realized that I had a problem.

The typical weight for a 9-year-old boy at 4'4" is between 60-80 pounds. At 165.7, I was not just overweight. The dangers associated with obesity include decreased lifespan, Type II

Diabetes, heart disease and cancer. I was also at a higher risk of developing asthma and other health problems. I knew none of this at the time, only that I didn't want my identity to be shaped by my weight. I began taking responsibility for my excessive eating instead of making excuses. I stopped eating double and triple meals. At dinner or lunch, instead of eating 2-4 servings I cut back to 1 or 2. I also replaced a few of my daily 4-6 hours of television time with outdoor activities.

I started playing my first recreational sport, soccer, that year. Even though I was not that good at soccer, and I didn't love the sport, it got me out of the house and active. I enjoyed being a part of a team, and they relied on my strengths such as my strong kick. This came in handy when I was playing defense and I took pride every time the coach chose me to take a penalty kick. I was still overweight, but I was heading in the right direction. I can't lie, I still counted down the minutes until halftime where I would scarf down as many orange slices as possible. But, orange slices are lot healthier than powdered doughnuts.

After the soccer season ended, I joined a baseball team. This was the first time my size gave me a competitive advantage and where I found my passion for sports. I was quickly recognized as the best hitter on the team and my teammates looked up to me as a talented player. This gave me a newfound sense of confidence and gave me hope that I could shift my identity from the overweight kid to a skillful athlete.

With a few seasons of soccer and baseball under my belt and less heavy than I had been, I decided to try out for football. Football was the most strenuous exercise yet as it included two workouts a day in the summertime incorporating weight training, conditioning and high intensity football related drills. Often, these drills would put me on the spot with the entire team watching, exposing any weaknesses. This motivated me to take my weight training and conditioning off the field seriously. I wanted to hold my own. Sophomore and junior year I had been content with the progress I had made, but in comparison to other athletes, I really didn't stand out. The summer going into my senior year, I started exercising on my own in addition to team trainings. I would jog to a small beach by my house and run sprints. I was eating even healthier and paired with the number of calories I was burning; my fat was melting away. I ended up playing three sports in high school and winning "Defensive Player of the Year" on my football team. I went on to play collegiate football before that got cut short due to an injury.

Unfortunately, the injury was largely due to being overweight in my younger years. Though I had overcome obesity, the impacts it had on my body and my ability to play sports have been lasting. My hips were so damaged from carrying excessive weight that it was likely I would need a hip replacement before age 25 if I continued to play.

Though my sports career ended, my healthy lifestyle did not. During my physical transition, I also experienced a mental one. My image of myself had transformed from "fat" to "fit" and I was no longer defined and limited by an unhealthy weight.

I am now a fitness enthusiast and health nut, eager to help others who want to undergo a similar transition. I have started Fitness Native for this sole purpose, connecting people who are excited to get in shape with personal trainers and gym owners who can help make this a reality. I coined the term Fitness Native from my own personal experiences, as a person who has been transformed physically and mentally through the power of fitness and healthy eating. With 1 in 3 children in the United States struggling with obesity, I have also launched a Fitness Native campaign which donates 20% of all proceeds to multiple charities supporting the prevention of obesity.

My experiences have taught me that your biggest obstacle can become your biggest success. I look at my struggle with obesity as a blessing which has shaped my love for the fitness world. This summer, 14 years after I stepped on the scale as a fourth grader weighing 165.7 pounds, I am living and working in Thailand. My days are no longer measured in food, but in building Fitness Native, snorkeling in coral reefs and hiking waterfalls. Now twenty-two years old, my breakfast consists of natural spirulina protein smoothie bowls from my favorite cafe instead of sugar-coated cereal and Pop-tarts. Double-cheeseburgers and French fries have been replaced by steamed vegetables, meat and fish. I no longer feel like a grounded Superman, but one whose possibilities are endless.

* * * * *

What I Became When I Grew Up

Teresa Cristina Holden

On September 6, 1983, I was initiated into a whole new realm of being: senior kindergarten. It was the first day where I was in the spotlight; under the microscope. My mother did not work outside our home, and so I had never been to daycare or even had a babysitter before. I had been raised, or I should say coddled, by her for the first 5 years of my life. She was my best friend. Yes, I had a doting dad and two older sisters but Mommy was my confidante. The kindergarten classroom was filled with pint size strangers. Broken routine. Weird smells. Lots of loud people. Boxed lunches... The outside world was an uneasy place. Change was unfair to a five-year-old, but necessary.

It was my kindergarten teacher, Miss Downs, who first asked her bright-eyed, innocent students that pivotal question. "Teresa, what do you want to be when you grow up?"

It was the most significant question ever posed to a human being in one's lifetime. Well, at least that is what it felt like to 5-year-old me. She would have been better off asking me to explain the Theory of Relativity ... I was not in the mood to play along. I was confused. My mind raced. My face turned beet red. Silence.

Other children exclaimed, "Fireman!" "Nurse!" or "Policeman!"... I was tongue tied. How were they so sure? Now that I reflect upon it, I think only the extroverts blurted out something, just to appease the teacher. I was a shy, introverted little girl with rich and deep emotions on the inside.

For my remaining grade school years, I was charged with the great responsibility of knowing my life path. It was a fully loaded concept. Doctor? Lawyer? What? Somehow, I just could not picture myself doing either. They were fancy titles that had no meaning to me. The only thing I really knew with certainty was that I liked to help people. I liked to share with them the things I knew so they would know them too. I liked it when people would smile at me, and I would smile back. I enjoyed making people happy. Making them feel happy when they were sad; feel comforted when they were hurt. I was always befriending those who had nobody to hang out with. On quite a few occasions, I was playfully called "Mother Teresa." I did not mind. She was a superb role model for humanity.

While in high school, personality tests imposed by guidance counsellors revealed that I was placed in the 'idealist' category. That was a fancy way of saying that I "would benefit from meaningful contribution in my career where my values could be upheld." True. It was called the True Colors personality test. It worked. Then the Myers-Briggs test confirmed that I was the 'counsellor idealist' type. I knew these assessments were accurate, because I had consistently been scolded to 'get real' and to take off my rose-colored glasses. I had also been subjected to teasing because I saw the world differently. Even my mother teased me about my rare world views, calling me "Pollyanna." This rare personality was somewhat of a challenge. What was a girl to do? My optimism was boundless, but so was my naiveté. I could be a minister, counsellor, or a social worker. These were all closer, yes, to the ideal, but I was still not convinced. I kept searching.

Then came the OJ Simpson trial, televised on CNN. The lead prosecutor Marcia Clark became my role model quickly. She was smart, professional and educated. The law profession became appealing at that time because of her. I then became involved in a mock trial and starred as the lead prosecutor at my school. I was an instant star! I was affectionately called

Marcia, as I had the curly brown hairdo and no-nonsense attitude to match.

But I was redirected again, as I realized that law school promised to be yet another drudgery. Three additional years of study stacked onto my already completed four? That would not work. My corporate-lawyer uncle also advised me on course content, which seemed a little on the dry side compared to a Hollywood portrayal of Law and Order. No offense meant to the lawyers out there, but lawyers do not have the best reputation for being nice. Also, any personality test would show I would be on the wrong path!

To my surprise, teaching became my "thing" through an appointment teaching at a private school. What started out as a side job to supplement my master's degree, turned out to be a tremendously eye-opening experience. The teaching stint did not end there. In fact, the stint turned into a long-running sitcom. Well, some moments felt like I was putting on a show entertaining about fifty twenty-year-old's. Some days attempting to keep their attention was difficult but I managed. It was one of my gifts. I was a part-time English teacher. Students loved my teaching approach. This experience helped cement for me how natural it was for me to be around people.

When September rolled around, so did college orientation. This time I was at the head of the class. I was no longer a student; rather, a professor! Yes! A faculty appointment was one of the bigger moments of my life. My university education had paid off... Mom and Dad were proud! It was a dream job! I was working 20 hours a week and lecturing to a few hundred students at a time. It was the moment for me to shine. It was exactly what I wanted to do; mentoring, creating curriculum, contributing to people's academic lives. Lecture halls and grading papers, nominations for teaching excellence. I was at the top of my game and in my prime. Hmm... was this new career, 'The Career?' Was it the answer to my kindergarten teacher's question, "What do you want to be when you grow up?" Was this the one?

However, the global recession arrived and an ugly reality settled in. Being in contract roles under a union in a small town, the axe was bound to fall. Layoffs came rushing down the metaphorical hallway and that tidal wave drowned me. Without a prior word of warning, the Associate Dean told me that everything that I had worked for would no longer be of value to them. My thick portfolio of teaching evaluations and awards might as well have been dumped into a shredder. I had poured 9 years of my life into this career and somehow, I thought I was guaranteed a professorship. This shook me to the core. I was devastated. Change was unfair but necessary once again.

Discouraged and hurt, I turned to my best friend and bastion of support: my husband Ryan. His confidence in me was immense. He was proud of me, whatever my efforts and accomplishments were. I also looked upward. God was there for me and so was my strong faith. Funnily enough, what followed might have been God's way of affirming the end of my teaching career.

One month later, I had miraculous news: my two-year-old son Christian would soon be getting a new baby brother or sister! I discovered I was pregnant again, and my husband and I were ecstatic. Despite having hit a professional low point, I was overjoyed with being a mother once again. My family grew spiritually amidst these unpredictable times. I put my energy towards having a healthy pregnancy and being a hands-on stay-at-home mother. Motherhood is the best because it is a role you can never quit or be fired from! It is an ongoing dedication and labor of love. It is my full-time job with no days off or sick days! It is a blessing and sometimes it is challenging, but it is my destiny. I used every last ounce of my nurturing, compassion, love, and care giving skills to my beautiful children. I felt like the richest person in the world as a mother! I was rich. I was complete. Motherhood is something that nobody could ever buy.

I would never have traded my new baby boy, Dominic, to keep my teaching job. Parenthood is the ultimate career. Being "Mommy Teresa" was fulfilling in its own unique way, and I kept writing and building my life portfolio. That was the only portfolio that matters.

Career breakdown was just an opportunity for redirection. It was a period in my life where I was forced to transition. It was difficult, sometimes painful but I got through it. I had thought that staying at the college was the best professional move, but God had greater plans for me! I started researching about finding one's purpose in life.

When you believe that you are in no way wealthy, you must think about the personal satisfaction you can gain by reframing your priorities. My priorities have proven to be about the people I love: my family. All the while, I have kept my fundamental optimism. Although sometimes it was difficult to cut through the fog, I saw the beacon of light. I understood my primary role was to be a mother at heart and provide nurturance to humanity. That meant I should work to encourage people; to lift them up, to support them. Share with others my life lessons. It is my authentic gift.

"What did you become when you grew up?" now has a variety of answers for me. I will try to put on all my hats: teacher, motivational speaker, philosopher, mentor and writer. I am also a wife and mother. All of the above. That is what I became when I grew up.

* * * * *

Two Dollars a Slice

Kalpesh (Kal) Patel

I live in Mason, Ohio with my amazing wife of 20 years, Lina, and my two beautiful teenage daughters. At age 45, I feel incredibly lucky and blessed to be the President and CEO of two companies that I founded myself - Crestpoint Inc. and 1st Inspection Services, Inc. I am also a co-owner of NewGen Ohio and a few other companies. This is part of my story.

I remember hearing stories from my grandmother about my dad who grew up in a small village outside of Surat in the state of Gujarat. She had raised my father on her own, as my grandfather had passed away when my father was only a few years old. My grandfather was a farmer and he left her some land. My grandmother continued to work on the farm, and had enough money to send my father to college. He got married at the early age of 26 and decided that in order to break the family tradition of "working the farm," he had to do something drastic. He left just shortly after I was born in 1972 to head to America, the Land of Opportunity. He left his entire family - his mother, his wife, and his three children - to find opportunity. My father first moved to Canada and worked many jobs save enough money for airline tickets to have us join him. Once we were settled in Canada, my mother and father both worked while my grandmother took care of us. We lived there until 1976, when we joined the hotel business in California. My father had acquired a 30-room independent hotel for $100,000, and we lived on site. Thus, began life in America. Two years later we moved again, this time into a 16-room independent motel that my father bought for $130,000 in the small-town of Vinita, Oklahoma.

I remember going to school in the 2nd grade where none of the kids had ever met someone from India. I vividly recall the kids asking me "What tribe are you from?" when I told them I was Indian. It was an adjustment growing up in such a homogeneous environment. I was ridiculed many times as most of the kids were ignorant of other cultures. Growing up as part of the only Indian family in a small town of seven thousand was tough. Other motel owners in the area had "American Owned" signs posted outside of their motels. It was very confusing to me. We were Americans, but were treated as foreigners and discriminated against quite often. As we adjusted to the "American" lifestyle, there were still many other challenges. since our family owned a motel and we lived on site, we could not invite friends over to hang out in the backyard or play in the neighborhood. I would find myself riding my bike to my friends' homes and we would hang out at their houses. This bothered me a lot at the time, but looking back, I feel like the difficulties encountered during those times helped me understand how to navigate through almost any situations that come my way.

As early as age 8, my brother, sister and I helped our parents with all the tasks related to running a small independent motel; everything from making up rooms, taking care of landscaping and maintenance related items, to renting rooms to guests. Every morning before we got on the bus to go to school, we had chores to do. I was responsible for taking out the garbage from newly-vacated guest rooms, my brother took out the towels and sheets, and my sister cleaned the furniture and ran the vacuum. This was a huge life lesson in work ethic, teamwork, and the ability to achieve if you put forth the effort. Now, don't get me wrong - I complained all the time to my parents about how my friends didn't have to do this kind of stuff, and my father always told me "If you don't like living here, you are welcome to move in with your friends." Trust me, I thought about it many times, but I never did it. I didn't know then that I would need those lessons, and now I am so glad that I stuck with it.

At the end of the day, I have always wanted to be an entrepreneur, I just didn't know it. Everyone around me was going to school to become engineers, doctors, or lawyers. My parents wanted me to follow the rest of my peers, perhaps to spare me all the hard work and uncertainty involved in becoming a successful entrepreneur. Therefore, I decided to become a dentist. I started by taking some prerequisite classes and found out quickly that the medical field was not my calling. I just simply did not enjoy what I was learning, and knew I wouldn't be satisfied with my career unless I was passionate about what I was doing.

It was then when I realized that I had discovered my true passion back in the eighth grade, I just didn't know it at the time. You see, back then my parents would give me $2 for lunch every day. However, I got tired of eating the same old lunch from the cafeteria and decided to save my lunch money for the entire week. The following week I ordered a pizza and had it delivered to the school at lunch. Quickly, I was surrounded by my peers, all of them asking for a slice of my pizza. Of course, I willingly complied, but asked for $2 a slice in return. I ended up selling the entire pizza (ten slices) and doubled my investment of $10. More importantly, I was filling the obvious needs of the kids around me while supporting the local pizza joint. I was an entrepreneur.

I got married in 1997 and moved to Fort Collins, Colorado where I opened a t-shirt shop downtown with a loan from friends and family. I borrowed $30,000 from some people close to me so that I could begin my future as an entrepreneur. My wife found a job in Denver, so we had to relocate from Fort Collins. I continued to operate the shop by commuting three hours round trip every day until mid-1998. I was coming home to Denver on Interstate 25 one beautiful sunny day, when the driver of a car on the other side of the highway lost control, went through the median and hit me head on. I remember getting out of my car and a few people rushing over telling me to lay down. My car had rolled over four times and I had injured my head and ear. It took me about two months to recover from these injuries and gave me time to really think about what was important to me in life. At that point, I decided to sell the shop because it wasn't worth the risk of driving back and forth every day. I sold the shop for just enough to break even and went to work for a department store in Denver.

In 1999, I decided to get into the hotel development business with three friends. I found some land in Castle Rock, Colorado, built a 64-room hotel and opened in early 2000. I was the General Manager, as well as the maintenance engineer, front desk manager, accounting department, etc. This was not what I had envisioned when I went into the hotel development business. Approximately a year and a half later, things weren't going as anticipated with the hotel or the partnership. I was asked to leave my general manager position, but stayed on as an investor until late 2001, when my shares were diluted in the hotel and I lost over $150,000. I started to get this feeling that maybe the hotel business was not what I was meant to be doing.

With an enormous amount of debt, in 2001 my wife and I moved to Cincinnati to live with my brother. I began working as a general manager at a fitness club, where I met a personal trainer named Craig Auberger. We got to know each other well, and would go for coffee almost every day after work. He became my mentor and helped me get a better understanding of who I was and what I was trying to accomplish. This is when things really started making more sense for me. After he introduced me to home inspections, I went to work for a company as an inspector. I realized within a few months that I had to start my own company. In 2003 Craig and I started our own home inspection business, with two additional inspectors. In the beginning things were great.

On August 9, 2004, I fell off a roof as I was doing an inspection - a fifteen foot drop onto concrete that completely shattered my right wrist and broke several bones in my right arm. This was just five days before my wife was due with our second daughter, and just sixteen months after my first daughter was born. Every day, I am grateful for my wife who is amazingly tough and has been by my side through it all. I can honestly say I wouldn't be where I am today without her. The nine surgeries required over the next three years to repair my injuries were probably the best things that could have happened to me at that point. I realized then that I had to work on the business, and not in the business. I began the business of franchising our home inspection company, and the company is growing as a result.

Looking for something that would feed my passion for starting new businesses, I decided to get back into hotel development. In 2008, I found a piece of land in Columbus, Ohio and, along with two friends, began the development arm of a new hotel company. We didn't want to get involved in the day-to-day management side of the hotel business, so we found a joint venture partner whose company would operate the hotel once it was built. One day, I was speaking with Jed Sherman, another friend of mine from my fitness gym days. As we talked, I was reminded of his experience as an operations manager and his interest in day-to-day operations. I was able to convince him to move from Virginia to Ohio to help launch the management division of our new company.

Through some intensive marketing and networking efforts, within a few months another lender appointed us as the receiver for another hotel. Soon after that we were appointed receiver for five more hotels. Meanwhile, we were contacted by other hotel owners whose properties were having difficulties. They were looking for some third-party management to assist them. By 2014, we were successfully running both sides of the company, development and management, and expanding our office. During this period, we were also assisting buyers and sellers of hotels, and opened the real estate brokerage arm of the company.

When I look back at the so-called "tragedies" in my life, they were pivotal points that helped guide me in the right direction. I always say that "Everything happens for a reason. We just don't know at the time what the reason is, but we have to patiently wait and we will know when the time is right."

The one thing that gets you through life is "Grit." It embodies my parents, and it describes me. Whatever you do in life you must do it with passion - find the passion and add some "Grit," and the results will be unbelievable success. Keep in mind that what success means to you and what it means to me are different. If you and only you define your success, you will be successful.

So, you ask "What is Kal's success?"

It's now 2017 and we have 14 hotels in our portfolio with four under construction and three more in the pipeline for 2018. Half of the hotels are owner-operator properties, and the other half are third party development/management. The inspection company is currently at seven locations in three states, and our brokerage has successfully transacted several hotel deals. Both of my daughters have been jumping rope for years with a team in Mason, Ohio called The Comet Skippers. There are over seventy jumpers on the team which travels locally, nationally and internationally, and I am honored to be an Assistant Coach.

The real success for me is how I have impacted the people who are part of the 1st Inspection franchises, the investors and owners of the hotels, the employees and team members in each of these businesses and all of the jumpers that are part of The Comet Skippers. If I have had a way to change someone's life in a positive way through inspiration, motivation and support, then "I am successful."

* * * * *

Not Quite Ivy League

Anne Skinner

"A Truly Wealthy Woman is one whose children run into her arms when her hands are empty"
~ *Anonymous*

I was born with a passion for people, to show love and compassion in all encounters, and above all else to always do what is right. I've always been a believer in dreaming big, and in helping others grow to be their very best and most authentic self. I guess deep down I've always wanted to be a counselor, coach and speaker. I realize now that I have been all those things since a very young age, and multiple times I've been drawn to travel and study with some of the greatest thought leaders of our times. Through the ebbs and flows of life, I now find that all my experiences, good or bad, were preparing me for "a time such as this." Somehow the circle of life answered my soul's deepest desires to make a difference, to be the change in the world. I am a Transformational, Executive and Financial Coach; a catalyst for authentic living and lasting change, which ultimately sends ripples out and encourages growth and change in all those I work with, and those their lives touch.

Life has thrown me a million curveballs and I have often taken myself off track, been forced to regroup and course correct. I know that since I was very young, each and every detour, each encounter and mishap, came wrapped with silver linings. The people I was meant to meet and lessons that I needed to learn, were all experiences that would help me to help others facing the same challenge. Most of all, all of this has made me who I am today.

I was raised in what looked like a perfect family, but was in reality, filled with pain, anger, secrets and judgement. I loved and cared for them all deeply, yet I constantly day-dreamed. I dreamed of a perfect life filled with unconditional love, joy, laughter, a fulfilling successful career, a house full of happy children and yes, a Prince Charming charging in on his white horse to save me. Yet still, not knowing any better, my childhood rose-colored glasses helped me believe that in all the chaos, pain, and lack, I was already living a wealthy life. Since forever, I would write and draw pictures of the big beautiful home on the ocean, a fancy sports car, and a larger car and driver in my wrap around driveway in the front of my home. I dreamed big and never thought for one minute that I would not have all of this and more. I believed in myself and my dreams, and most of all I felt it to my core that I would never stop until I had created and was living the peaceful, fulfilling life I had spent my youth dreaming of.

Well, as the Rolling Stones would say:
"You can't always get what you want...
but if you try sometimes...
well you just might find, you get what you need"

As my life went on, I may not have always gotten what I was seeking at the time. But often, when it was time for me to let go or learn a new lesson, they came as gentle as a cool summer breeze or fierce as a tornado. Each time, much of what I knew of my life was challenged, shattered and inevitably replaced by what the Universe had for me next. It has been and continues to be a hero's journey of exploration, growth and learning to always bring the light and love, even in the darkest times.

I was raised in Detroit, Michigan. From a very young age I would go to work with my mother on weekends and when I had days off school. Mom ran the main office of St. Vincent

DePaul in downtown Detroit; feeding, clothing and helping the poor and lost. I went to strict Catholic schools for 12 years, and though my memories of my youth are very few and far between, I know I grew up in a life filled with dysfunctional love, anger, anxiety and fear. My heart has always longed to "fix" everyone, to make my family into that perfect family I dreamed of, to be loved and cared for the way I saw in my friends' families. I longed to take some of the burden away from my parents and siblings, so everyone could feel and know the peace, love, unity and happiness I wanted for all of us. My parents were children of the depression and both had experienced devastating family events when they were young. I knew they loved me and being very empathic, I swear I could feel the pain they tried to hide.

Being the youngest of 4, I never really understood how dysfunctional and poor our family really was. With 6 of us living in an 850-square-foot home, I knew we weren't rich, but I always had what I needed and wanted. I never suspected that we were poor; the people I helped my mom serve were so much worse off than my family and I were. In 2005 my mother passed, and in the few years following her death conversations with my older sister made me realize how poor we really had been.

Looking back on my childhood, I see how God was always there protecting me, teaching me and showing me how to see the good in everyone and in every situation. I learned how to keep my dreams alive, and to always strive for more and better for myself and others. I also see how I was always being taught, prepared and strengthened for the journey I was headed for. Besides working at St Vincent DePaul, my mother sold encyclopedias and, from a very young age, she took me to her sales training meetings. When we were at home or in the car, she often had on personal development greats such as Earl Nightingale, Dale Carnegie, Napoleon Hill and others.

162

This would be key in my developing a belief in myself, my drive to succeed, grow, inspire others and ability to face adversity head on...and for this I AM MOST GRATEFUL!

At the age of 17, however, I was given a great blow to my belief in myself, my goals and dreams.   My plans were to attend Dartmouth College and become a therapist and teacher for autistic children, using music as part of their therapy.   I accelerated my high school studies and graduated in 3 years, thinking it would save my parents money that they could put towards my college tuition.   I was so very excited and proud of myself when the acceptance letter from Dartmouth arrived; all my dreams were coming true. I was on my way. Life was magical!

When I told my parents my plan, they laughed and said, "That's great, but you're not going to Dartmouth. If you want to go to college, you will live at home, continue to work and go to Wayne State in downtown Detroit."

My dream was shattered by reality. I was in shock, "What do you mean? I've been accepted to Dartmouth, this is my plan, this is what I am doing!" From there it's all a blur; I was crushed, my belief in 'do what is necessary and you can have what you want' had blown up in my face. I was confused and lost.

My brother, who was attending Wayne State, took me to visit the campus and talk to an admissions advisor. This helped me about as much as throwing a live grenade into the rest of my dreams. Excitedly I told him of the degrees I wanted to pursue and what I planned to do with them. He went on and on that it was a horrible field to go into... that I would be in school for at least 10 years... and when I got a job the pay would be minimal... yep, there went the last bits of my *"Life's Passion, Purpose & Plan"*.

Have you ever been lost, completely without a vision or plan, feeling like everything you knew had been stripped away and you couldn't even see to tomorrow? Have you been in that place in your mind, where your future was all laid out on a whiteboard when you went to bed, but when you awoke someone had wiped it clean without leaving a clue? Are you aware that this place is what Buddhist Monks seek? I once explained a period of my life like this to a Monk and he said, "My Dear, that is what we call enlightenment and what we seek through meditation and reflection."

Well, I can tell you that if anyone had told me, "This is enlightenment," when my dreams and goals were taken away, I'd have called them a fool. I was lost, I was confused and I found myself with no direction or purpose. I took a couple of night classes at the local community college, worked full time at a local car dealership and part time as a dental assistant. I was lost and felt so all alone. About that time, I met a guy at work and began to date him. I spent as much time away from home as possible - working, with friends or dating. I was really looking forward to my 18th birthday when I planned to take a vacation to California to see friends, find a new job and a place to live. My fears got the best of me and I didn't stay in California, so soon as I returned home I began looking for a place to rent with a high school friend.

My friend backed out on me at the last minute, but I was determined to get out on my own. Having no other options at the time, I moved in with the guy I was dating. Three years later, I was a very successful weight loss clinic manager and leader in company sales. As successful and independent as I was, my family was treating me poorly for "living in sin." To prove them wrong, I once again went against my better judgement and married just before my 21st birthday.

The year I turned 25, I gave birth to my 3rd child. I had a 3-year-old boy, a 15-month-old girl and a newborn baby girl, and as much as I didn't believe in divorce, I knew that it was inevitable in the very near future. I needed to keep myself and my children safe from an abusive, alcoholic, drug addict. Having nowhere to go, I did all I could to keep us safe and worked hard in my home-based business for the next 6 years, working my way to district manager. The final quarter before everything changed, my team was 2nd highest in the nation, and my personal sales were at #1.

The day after the divorce, he tried to kill me. Then, he continued to grow more violent and angry with me and with the children when they stayed with him. It became imperative that I get myself and my children safely out of this dangerous situation. So, I packed up my 3 young children, walked away from my business, my family, friends and all I had ever known. I moved across the country from Michigan to Florida, as a single mom, all the way to the sunshine state with no job, and no friends, but the strong belief in myself and in God's protection and gentle guidance along the way.

In the early 90's the internet wasn't available to anyone but IBM and a few other large companies, cellphones were expensive and the size of a shoebox, long distance calls and shipping were all too much money for me to keep my business going long distance.

So, here I was in a beautiful location, in my dream home with my 3 kids. This was not just a new chapter in my life, this was a new book! I was in this 'Buddhist Enlightenment place' and this time I have to say it did feel a bit like a fairy tale, or a superhero's triumph. I had a new place to call my home and once again love and nurture my children into the beautiful unique, brilliant individuals that they were intended to be.

Since continuing my Michigan business in Florida was unrealistic, it was time to create a new direction for my career. I looked at all the skills I had gained over the years and all the work I had done, and set out to find a new course that would support my family and be flexible enough so I could always be there for my children. It was definitely divine intervention when I was in the running for a regional director of marketing position for an outpatient therapy company. Once they narrowed it to 3 candidates, part of the interview process was to put together a marketing plan overview, which I had never done. I wanted this job badly and it was such a great fit for me, so I worked diligently and put together a very comprehensive marketing plan.

The night before I was to present my plan, I woke up in the middle of the night with a great idea for a slogan. I jumped out of bed and changed the cover adding an awesome slogan and logo! Though the other two candidates had much stronger qualifications, the company loved my slogan and wanted it; I got the job and began my career in the Florida healthcare industry. In the many years here in Florida, I have been blessed with opportunities that always gave me the finances needed to raise my children in a comfortable lifestyle, the flexibility to be available for them when they needed me and to attend their events and activities, increasing career advancement, and many great experiences, social events and travel over the years.

Being a single mom of 3, there wasn't much time for more than work and family, but my executive positions in marketing, business development and sales allowed me great friendships, personal development, southeast travel and socializing as part of my job description. The crooked road from successful network marketing business owner to VP of business development and director allowed me to experience fulfillment in many areas of my life. Though there were many tough times, I was blessed to give my children a great home, life and college educations. I've done my best to be a responsible, loving mom and my greatest reward has been raising my 3 fabulous, now successful adult, children all on my own. They are all married now and have given me 3 beautiful granddaughters - no greater gifts could I ask for.

My family has always come first, but as the years have passed and they've moved away, and my parents passed on, I realized it was time to remember who I was. Time to reopen and explore my hopes, my dreams, my authentic gifts and what brings me joy. I finally gave myself permission to go after my dreams, stand in my truth and not let others define or influence me. I am living a fulfilling life on my terms, using my unique skills, knowledge and lessons-learned to coach and educate others. Together we create strategic life, career and financial plans, identify what holds them back, and developing strategies to overcome the obstacles. I am helping them grow into their most authentic self and live their greatest life too.

Even through the ups and downs, I love my life and the authentic me that now shows up each and every day. My greatest *"Wealthy Living"* is having the courage to live my authentic life and have the time and money freedom to be with my loved ones anytime and anywhere I want.

Now, I am Living a Wealthy Life and you can too!

> *"You aren't wealthy until you have something that money can't buy"*
>
> ~ *Garth Brooks*

One False Step

Ryan Nicley

In today's busy, high-tech, always-connected world, we sometimes lose sight of what's truly important in life. Too many times we are faced with tragedy before we wake up and begin to appreciate the simple things that have been there all along. I was recently reminded of this on a family Spring Break trip to Asheville, North Carolina.

I consider myself an outdoorsman; and I enjoy camping, fishing, kayaking, hiking and just about anything that involves the outdoors. It's been important for me to introduce my kids, Jack (12) and Addi (10), to the outdoors and try to instill in them an appreciation for nature. We have had many adventures as a family and made many great memories. I know my children will fondly look back on them, as I do on my childhood memories. However, on our trip to Asheville, we experienced an unplanned adventure that we will all remember for the rest of our lives.

It all started with a typical family visit to the Mile High Swinging Bridge at Grandfather Mountain. Being the outdoorsman that I am, and always looking for that added adventure, I suggested we park in the Hikers' Lot and hike the almost-half-mile Bridge Trail up to the Swinging Bridge. This was a moderate climb up a fairly easy trail, taking only about 15 minutes to reach the bridge. The trail switched back and forth through the mixed hardwood forest, boulders and rock faces. The whole family chatted all the way up about how amazing the views were.

When we reached the bridge, there was a brief discussion to try and coerce my wife and daughter to cross the bridge, but my son and I were not successful. My wife and daughter are a little afraid of heights so they decided to stay back near the visitor's center until my son and I returned. They sat on some boulders near the bridge so they could watch us and still enjoy the beautiful views. Jack and I crossed the bridge and continued to climb up to the highest point we could find (as boys will do) to take in the view and a get a couple pictures. My son and I only stayed on the other side of the bridge for maybe 10-15 minutes and then returned to meet back up with my wife and daughter. We were all still very excited from the success of our short hike, and decided to try another trail or two before we left. The trailhead was just a short walk across the parking lot at the visitor's center. That's where the real adventure began.

First, I must set the stage for this adventure and share our lack of preparedness for what we were about to encounter. We had not expected anything too strenuous, and therefore did not have any supplies with us other than a single bottle of water I was carrying. In addition, we were all wearing regular gym shoes instead of adequate hiking shoes.

We started off on Grandfather Trail and we picked up the fun right where we had left off on the Bridge Trail. The rock faces, cliffs, boulders and views were breathtaking. The trail was a little more strenuous than the Bridge Trail, but this was very similar terrain and nothing too terribly difficult. My wife and I are in pretty good shape and, of course, the kids never get tired when they are having fun. We walked along the trail and continued taking photos, chatting and talking about how awesome it was. We were making great memories and loving every minute of it. I could not have been happier to be sharing something I love (the outdoors and hiking) with my family. The fact that they were enjoying it as much they were, made it even more special.

We had found a map of the trails online and chose a planned route that, according to the map legend, included a ladder. We didn't exactly know what to expect, but we knew there was a ladder on the trail that we were going to have to climb at some point. We left the Grandfather Trail and headed up the Underwood Trail (where the ladder was located). The terrain of the Underwood Trail was similar to what we had experienced, but the climb was getting a little steeper. Things were getting a little more strenuous, but nothing crazy.

Well, nothing crazy until we reached the ladder. We literally had to climb straight up the face of a cliff on a ladder made from 4x4's. There were no safety rails or anything like that; just a simple wooden ladder and a sheer drop off the mountain on the left side. As we stood there contemplating this ladder, I could see my wife, and I, both became a little nervous. There was nothing safe about what we were getting ready to do, but it seemed like it could be a manageable challenge, so up we went. Once we made it up the ladder, the adrenaline was rushing. You should have seen the smiles on everyone's faces. I think we were all amazed at what we had just accomplished. More than likely, my kids were thinking: *I can't believe Mom and Dad just let us do that!* After a few pictures and thumbs up, onward we went.

By this time, we were all having a blast, laughing and talking about how awesome this was and thinking pretty highly of our hiking skills and abilities. We had no idea what still lay ahead of us. The Underwood Trail reconnected with Grandfather Trail, and just as we reached MacRae's Peak (at 5,845 feet elevation) the clouds started to get darker, the wind picked up noticeably and it began to rain lightly. We quickly ducked into a rock crevice to keep dry and figure out what we were going to do. Although we were still laughing at this point, our awesome, exciting adventure had just turned very scary for me. We huddled up against the rocks for maybe 10 minutes, but I knew we needed to keep moving for fear of the storm getting worse. For a moment, I panicked a little inside, thinking to myself: *What the hell have I gotten my family into and how am I going to get us off this mountain safely?*

Within about 10, or maybe 15 minutes, the rain stopped, but who knew for how long? We had to get off the peak of this mountain quickly. Just then, coming up over the rock face from the direction we had been hiking, we saw a young boy followed by his parents. He was probably 10 or so, and I remember thinking to myself: *If he just came over that rock face, it can't be that bad.*

I grabbed the family and said, "Let's go."

I walked up ahead to scout things out and was shocked by what I was about to take my family through. The "path" was literally a 3-foot wide shelf with a sheer drop on one side. We had to traverse that to get to the next ladder and the rocks were wet and slippery and the wind was still blowing pretty hard. As my daughter came over the rock and saw it, fear set in and she began to cry. In that moment, I thought the whole family was going to lose it and break down right there. However, I knew we had to move and it took 3 very long minutes to calmly assure them it would be ok but we had to move now. At that moment, I too was scared, but I knew we had to move. The wind was still blowing very hard and I was afraid it would blow one of my kids (especially my daughter) right off the mountain. Even though I was not 100% certain, I convinced them it would be ok and that we should go down the trail now before the rain started up again.

We progressed across the slippery, narrow shelf and made it to the ladder, or I should say, ladders. When we looked over the edge there were 5 ladders back to back that we would have to climb down. Keep in mind, these ladders were made of wood and were now wet from the rain. I was waiting for someone to slip off at any moment, but thankfully no one did.

In an effort to provide some sort of safety, I went down first so I could be below to help or catch the kids if need be. My wife helped them onto the ladders and then she came down last. We carefully climbed down the ladders one by one until we reached the forest floor and the normal trail.

At that point, I think we all felt an overwhelming sense of relief (I know I did) and everyone was expressing gratitude to be off the peak of that mountain and out of that situation. The mood quickly changed back to a much happier one, similar to what we had experienced during the early part of our hike; although, I could still sense an urgency to get back to the car. My son continually stopped to take pictures behind us and document what he had just been through (to share with his friends, no doubt), while my wife repeatedly called to him to hurry and keep walking. I think she was ready to get off the mountain. We continued our pleasant descent back down the mountain towards the car. There were a few cables and ropes we had to use as we went, as well as few more ladders, but nothing remotely close to what we experienced on Mac Rae's Peak. Although there was no canopy to protect us from the elements, the wind and rain had subsided by then. All was good again.

As we strolled down the trail towards the parking lot where our car was parked, we could not stop talking about what we had just experienced. In fact, it was pretty much the topic of conversation for the next few days. I reminded my family, as I always do, about how important it is to make great memories. They quickly reminded me that those might not be the kind of great memories they wanted to have, but we still got a good laugh out of it.

I'm not saying it's a good idea, or even necessary, to take your family on a strenuous hiking trail and risk death in order to make memories, but the whole experience reminded me of how important my family is to me. Sometimes it's our families and loved ones we end up taking for granted. We think they will always be there and they know how we feel about them. But they won't and they don't. Our loved ones are so very special and we should take every chance we get to spend time with them and make memories. In the end, those memories may be all you have.

Tristan's Time

James Savage

Relationships are built on words and actions. The smallest word or phrase can forever change your life and how you feel. An action that may seem small can either shake the foundations of someone's life, or make them stronger. Hearing a simple phrase like *"You are amazing,"* or *"I love you,"* especially from someone you love, can change how you look at yourself. Something as simple as buying a coffee for the person behind you in line, can change their horrible day to an amazing one. The littlest things can have the biggest impact.

Three years ago, my son Tristan was born and came in like a wrecking ball. His birth was a little thing that forever changed our lives. In my life before Tristan, I was building my own business, working five days a week from 8:00 AM until 6:00 PM. Usually, networking events took place in the evenings, and I would be out for long hours in order to grow the business. At the time, my wife and my business were the only things that mattered. My focus was on growing the business into an empire that would take care of me in my old age. I was even willing to travel over an hour away to take care of a client. At the time, my business was my baby and I treated it with kids gloves. After Tristan was born it all changed. I started cutting my time down at the office to three days a week, and two days at home with him. At first this arrangement was so we could save money on day care, but it quickly became something more.

It was early April 2014, when Tristan and I first started our tradition of being together every Thursday and Friday. I won't lie - as a new father, I was really scared at first, but the fear quickly went away as we developed a routine. Luckily, we started off with the relatively simple things like snuggles, feedings, changings, etc. There was a lot to do, but at least he wasn't mobile yet.

Now there was a new system in play: instead of working all the time, I was down to just three days a week and no more networking at night. In the beginning, it was hard to be caught between the feelings of needing to get work done and needing to focus on this little guy. It was tough to find a balance, but as Tristan and I began to get into a schedule, and get used to each other, we figured it out. I would answer e-mails when they came in, and call my employees and clients when he was down for naps. Every night when my wife came home, we would eat dinner as a family and then I would get to work with the reporting and social media. This new schedule forced me to be more laser focused and productive on a short time frame. It worked so well, we still keep close to the same schedule today.

Tristan and I spent a lot of time going shopping, to parks, and taking walks around our neighborhood to see the world. As the months went by, we got more settled into our routine. Every Thursday and Friday we would have talks, eat some food, and really get to know each other. When he was upset, we would sooth and figure out the problem, when he did something new we would cheer and bounce up and down on the thing he achieved.

In October of 2014 we moved back to Cincinnati for business and family reasons, and for a better place to raise Tristan. This is when life changed again - we moved in with my father and mother-in-law while we waited for our house to sell and we looked for another. Tristan was no longer in regular daycare at all, but in Grandma and Papa's daycare Monday through Wednesday, and with me on Thursday and Friday.

During the year we lived with my in-laws, my father-in-law was going through chemotherapy to recover from cancer. He had been in a cave stage, and Tristan was the source of him getting out and back into the world of the living. The funny thing about children - for better or worse, they don't let you rest. That's what Tristan did for his Papa: he kept him moving, laughing, and amazed! Every day as I worked upstairs, I could hear them downstairs playing and laughing.

Living with my in-laws had its ups and downs, although there were more ups than downs. The best thing about living with them was that it not only strengthened the bond they have with my son, but with me as well. We would have dinner every night together, play with Tristan together, and really grew closer as a family. They say it takes a village to raise a child, but I think it took a village to raise our family.

My wife and I also grew closer that year. We picked up some new habits from her parents that have improved our life and lifestyle. They are just small things, like tidying up Tristan's toys at the end of the day, and not watching television. The lack of TV gave us much more time to connect with each other and her parents. It was a true gift her parents gave us, and all of us have a better, stronger, and more honest relationship.

Tristan now had an extension to his world in a blink of an eye. Many of our friends and family believe that Tristan was the cure for my father-in-law's cancer. Here was a man who was hurting from chemo, and needing something as a distraction for his pain and sadness. Tristan came along and built up his world. My father-in-law is to this day, cancer free. We all believe that if Tristan wasn't there, my father-in-law would have had a harder time recovering. His grandson gave him something to live for, something to keep himself out of his own thoughts and continue to push through. Thankfully, we were there at the right time.

The best gift they could give Tristan was their time, and the best gift Tristan gave them was time. The bond they built is truly amazing. A child takes you out of your worries, your pain, and stress. You focus on them, and you don't have time for doubt and worry with a little one. They need your help and attention all the time, and can have the biggest impact on your life.

Tristan and I still spent every Thursday and Friday together. Now that we were in a new city, we took the time to explore. He was a little older, and growing up fast. We would go to parks, museums, zoos, and aquariums. Every week was full of new adventures that we would find around the city. During this time, I would work from home Monday through Wednesday when I wasn't in meetings or networking. I could hear everyone downstairs and would sneak down from time to time for a quick hug and hello. My days with Tristan were still the same, but since his grandparents were there I could answer the phone when an important call came in and I had to take a break. Thursday and Fridays are the best days of the week, because I spend time with my son, even if I have to work here and there.

One day in the fall of 2015, we were at the aquarium. Tristan was 21 months old and was walking by now. We had been there a few times before, but something happened that day that I will always remember. Tristan was walking through one of the tunnels with water and fish all around him, when I saw it - the wonder in his beautiful eyes at seeing the colors, the water, the fish swimming by, as if he was seeing it all for the first time. It made me stop and look at everything more closely, and was truly an amazing experience.

As Tristan grew, he became more independent at the playground and on our adventures. Watching him experience his first-ever climb up steps in the park by himself was terrifying and exciting for me at the same time. Every new sight, noise and experience was eye opening for him. And for me as well. It was like experiencing the world over again through the eyes of my two-year-old son. Watching him, I could see the joy in his eyes; it was like looking at the world for the first time. I saw ants again for the first time, I played with the soft sand again for the first time, and watched the sun go down again for the first time. We tend to take those little things for granted, but watching him experience them all was like experiencing it for the first time all over again.

As Tristan grew a little older, our life together got even better. Our bond grew deeper and deeper every day. I have experienced joy watching him do puzzles that are advanced for him, playing board games with him, and reading stories. Time goes by so fast with this little guy; we are learning together about the world each day and year. I learned that my life was boring without him and with him, my life is filled with more joy.

The other night, my son told me something he has probably said a hundred times over, but this time my heart caught in my chest. I was having a rough day at the office, was beating myself up, and Tristan walked up to me with his Captain American Toy. "I love you Daddy," he said. "Thank you for everything."

Though I had heard this many times over, this time I *heard* it. It took away all the troubles from my day, week, month, and year. Such a little thing that had a big impact.

It is time that allowed me to create this place in our relationship, something that comes with being lucky enough to run my own business and really know my own son. Bonds are built not in an instant, but over time and hard work on both ends. Everyday my father tells me he wishes he had done the same thing with his boys, and is happy for me that I can with mine. It's a rare gift and treat that I get to see my son grow and spend a lot of time with him. I am glad I have time, and though it goes by fast, I am very lucky to have it with Tristan.

Unexpected Journey

Allen (Big Daddy) Walker

As far back as I can remember I had always chased the almighty dollar. I can remember ordering flower seeds and selling door to door as a very young child, trying to find a way to become rich. I have consistently held at least one job since I was seven years old; there was just something about doing a good job and getting that cold hard cash. I will never know where this drive and desire came from but it has always been there.

With my outgoing personality and my desire to succeed, I found myself working in various MLM opportunities at the age of thirteen. Motivation tapes, sales tapes and records are an odd thing for a kid to be interested in, but these early years just drove me to want more. I learned early in childhood I could make money fast. I was only nine when I took care of Tennessee Walking horses and bailed hay for a family friend; then worked as a painter and a theatre usher when I was old enough to drive. I had done so many different things and held so many jobs because my mind was focused on making money quickly.

I was also focused on Linda Worstell, a cute young girl with gorgeous blue eyes, a great laugh and freckles with light brown hair. She took over my thought of money and being with her is all I could think of. At the age of 16, I found out I was going to be a father. I immediately married the love of my life and joined the Marine Corps to make sure I could pay for my child's birth and support my new family. After graduation, I was on my way to Parris Island, SC to go through 16 weeks of hell, so I could bring my child into the world without debt.

Leaping forward 5 years; I was medically discharged from the Marine Corps and had to find another way to make a living for my family. I found my first sales job and fell in love with selling cars and the money I could make. At the age of 22, I was making $80,000 a year and realized selling was where it was at. Here we were, at a very young age, buying a home, driving the latest and greatest hot cars, dining at the finest steak houses, and taking our children to expensive events. We had the world by the tail and we were running with it

This all came to a screeching halt on the 14th day of July in 1990. It was an event that changed my life forever. The day was beautiful; bright, sunny skies filled with fluffy white clouds. As I drove my family to the grocery store, we were in no hurry and were enjoying the drive. I decided to travel the scenic route and made a fateful right turn instead of sticking to our usual road. As we drove a couple of miles down Ohio State Route 131, a tree limb snapped from a dead tree and came crashing down on our car.

The impact was deafening as glass sprayed everywhere. Adrenaline fired up every nerve in my body as I fought to gain control of the car and get my family to safety. I glanced over and saw Linda was unconscious. I saw the gravel lot of a gas station up ahead and I quickly pulled in. A lady who had seen the accident ran up to the car as I pulled my children from the back. I asked her to "please take my kids away from the car," as I reached for the passenger side door.

As I opened the door it simply collapsed onto the road. I saw a huge gash in my wife's arm and noticed her skin tone was changing quickly. I immediately started CPR waiting for the ambulance arrive. After they took over from me, someone escorted me inside the gas station to tell me what I think I already knew, but hoped wasn't true. As several people physically braced me they informed me there was nothing they could do; Linda had passed away. My wife was gone.

I was lost, and now I had to inform my 5-year-old son, and his 2-year-old sister that their mother would no longer be in their lives. Everything we had bought and built didn't matter anymore; the money, the cars, the house. Who cares? The most important reason for me to succeed was gone. I still had my children, but the person that had been by my side since the age of 13 was gone. All the accomplishments, fun, and time spent sharing our deepest secrets and desires was washed away.

As time passed in my life, the rest of the decade of my 20's was lost. I spent so much time just trying to survive and help my two children live as normal a life as possible. At the end of that decade, I found myself working in the mortgage business and discovered a new source of my dream for wealth. We struggled through the slumps that came and went, but made a very comfortable living. Thanks to the lending laws passed by the United States Congress, the business of mortgage lending and home building exploded in the 2000's.

I managed a territory of three states for a national lending company, which had finally placed me in the top 1% of earners in Ohio. As my income multiplied and grew, so did my house, cars, trips, jewelry, clothes, and toys. You name it, we bought it. I had worked my entire life for this, and finally made it to the top. Little did I know, my time at the top wouldn't last very long. Since I worked for someone else, there was no way to ensure that this new-found success would continue.

One day, I received an email with information about a national conference call with all the Regional Managers and our direct reports. There was palpable excitement in the air as we started the phone call. We thought there was going to be an announcement about some major growth. We hoped many of us would be promoted to the next level so we could continue our ride to wealth. I certainly thought that was the case; after all, we had been riding high for a while. It only took about 3 minutes for this excitement to grow into a sick feeling in the pit of my stomach.

As the call was happening, we were all receiving knocks on our doors at home with the delivery of our pink slips. I received my last paycheck, without the bonus that had been earned and no severance package. I was living a $300,000-a-year life style that came to an abrupt end. The company was going down, the stock crashed very quickly, and what was considered our safety net quickly diminished to very little. Here I was, 40 years old, and suddenly out of a job. People in my field were blackballed from other careers and the stock market was taking a major hit. Lending of all kinds stopped and our entire economy came to a screeching halt.

For the first time in my life I had no plan, no idea what I was going to do with my life. How was I going to support my family? I soon realized I couldn't easily replace my income. One after the other, I lost my house, cars and the entire lifestyle that I had spent my entire life building. Soon everything was gone. I had believed that if I just worked hard enough and kept my credit strong, I would be successful. If this was success, I didn't want any part of it. It was a cruel and miserable joke that had no end in sight, and was in no way comical.

As I began to think about what had happen to my life plan, I soon started to understand that simply chasing the almighty dollar wasn't as fulfilling as I thought it would be. The relentless climb to the top left me empty. I regretted the time lost and the memories I missed making with my children and family. I decided it was time that I made a difference in the life of others, and maybe quit thinking about money all the time. So, after some research and thought, I realized I had education benefits from my military service that I could use to go to college. My plan was to be a special education teacher. I wanted to help others and make a difference. I had started to realize my legacy was nil. I hadn't really thought about others in my previous position. I had been more interested in just how much more money I could make by helping them reach their goal.

It was during the process of remaking myself that I started to live again. I would take the time to stop and talk with people at the coffee shop, the barber shop, and while having breakfast. These are some of my best memories in life to date. I learned so much, and met so many extremely engaging and interesting people that had done some miraculous things in their lives. I met World War II Vets, Korea and Vietnam Vets that spoke of the ugliness of war and how they managed to continue in life and take care of their families.

My new outlook also gave me more time to spend with a good friend whom I could talk with about life and the things we enjoyed. One of his passions was hosting Karaoke. Many times, I had attended his show, sang and enjoyed his entertaining ways. It wasn't long before he needed someone to fill in for him during a vacation, and he asked me if I would be willing. I was hesitant, as I really didn't know how to set up and control the equipment. My friend said, "It isn't tough to do. I can train you, and I think you will be great at it."

So, I trained for a few weeks on how to run the equipment and he took his vacation. The night went well, and the feedback he received about me were raving reviews. At his suggestion, I started working as a DJ while attending college at Xavier University to become a Special Education Teacher.

Music has been something I have enjoyed for as long as I can remember. My dad would always listen to Nat King Cole, Barbara Streisand, Sonny & Cher and country music. I grew up on skates at the Orbit One Roller Rink, and music was always a huge part of skating. I just didn't realize how this would all come together to change my life once again. If it hadn't been for music, I would have never made it through the years of mourning Linda and the horrible way that I lost her. And now, music was helping me make enough money to live on while attending college. That's exactly what I thought I had; just a side gig to get me through school. I was broke, and needed money for rent and groceries for myself and my children. I was making very little money, but I was learning to be happy. Little did I know that this "side gig" I had was going to send me on a journey to find my true calling.

Being a DJ has been the most fulfilling career of my life, and has provided me with many wonderful memories. It has introduced me to people I never thought I would meet and become friends with. Most importantly it brought to me a woman who has become my best friend, my comfortable place and the owner of our company. Debbie Rogers is an extremely important part in my success and happiness that I never knew was possible. I have learned to be happy with what I have and where I am, regardless of income, material goods or status. The best part is, building an organization that helps others reach their dreams and realize special moments, have made me feel so much more successful than I ever felt making a small fortune.

He Said, He Said; A Tale of Two Stories

Jeffrey Misner & Charlie Cottrelle

He Said: Jeffrey's Tale

I can picture the day like it was yesterday. My first day at Upper Canada College, and my home for the next 4 years.

Everyone felt like a stranger; as a brand-new 9th grader at my new school I didn't know anybody. I came from a school in a different part of the city, 35 kilometers away. At my old school, I was president of the student body, on every sports team and had friends since I was 4 years old. My new school had students that had been together since kindergarten. I was the new kid on the block - a position I had never experienced before. Then, I met Charlie Cottrelle.

He was a year younger- but had the same type of enthusiasm I was used to exhibiting. I could see the empathy in his eyes. I could hear the creativity of his humor. I could feel the genuine love he had for his friends. So selfishly, I knew I wanted to be his friend as well.

Luckily, it wasn't hard to establish a friendship. We both immediately joined the football team. I was a lineman; he was a defensive back. It didn't matter that we were in different grades or that he had a few inches on me. We were friends: plain and simple.

As we started getting immersed in other activities at our high school, we became a link of sorts for each other's grade. It was easy for my friends to become his and vice versa. We noticed how age was a weird, stereotypical determinant that usually led to friendships becoming stagnant within grades. Becoming an outlet for each grade was extremely important for us to foster our new relationships. Our friend Jack is my age, and has been a mentor of Charlie's for some time, and James is a younger version of myself that I would have never met without Charlie,

I was starting to notice the different but similar trends that made people like each other. Now there was a plethora of people to choose from, when deciding our peer groups. We basically created a larger ocean for each other's social lives. The best part was the ease with which it seemed to come about. I still hung out more often with friends in my grade, and Charlie did likewise. There is nothing like complaining about your next math test with your friends.

This relationship was further augmented when I became the Head of our Orange House - Howard's. There are 10 houses at Upper Canada, each one a group of 80 students. Intramurals, weekly meetings and mentor problems are the main facets of the house. The house system allows people to have a reason to socialize with other young men that wouldn't have done so otherwise. It was one of the first times I needed to leverage other people in reaching out to a mass audience. I had the role of mentoring 80 young men; something that seemed like an impossibility with my athletic, extra-curricular and academic calendars. I needed to rely on other senior members of the house to reach out to more junior members. Charlie was one of the guys I leaned on. He led his entire grade and became a focal point of the house.

This further expanded our abilities to reach mass audiences and build relationships with people from a multitude of backgrounds. The key was to get involved and learn as much about the other person as possible. We realized that people were scared to do exactly that. Not that they didn't want to - but because they lacked the knowledge or innate drive to do so. My mom is an elementary school teacher and I learned through her that getting people to talk about themselves is the best way to befriend them. Loyalty had always been the biggest factor in my friendships – which creates a natural urge for me engage in people's lives. I always loved learning about people.

What happened next was tragic. When I graduated Upper Canada College, I continued my education at the University of Southern California. The tragedy was not in the warm weather or freedom that came with being a student, but in Charlie and I losing touch with one another. I also lost touch with so many others that were still in Canada. Selfishly, I looked at my new situation as bigger and better- but quickly realized my mistake of dropping high school friends on my voyage to USC. My mistake was simple, but a repeat of a previous one. Just as I did when I left my junior high school for UCC, I forgot about the importance of close personal relationships. Even your best-friend-in-residence can't make up for the dozens of people who would drop whatever they were doing at a moment's notice to help you. That's what I left at UCC with Charlie and the realization came about a month and a half into the school year.

I was beginning to become frustrated or even angry with the lack of communication with my old friend. I made new friends in a variety of ways at USC: through hanging out in my residence, pledging my fraternity and joining clubs in the Business School. I followed the same formula that had led to my success at my previous "new experience", when I had joined the Blue Army at Upper Canada College (the name of the mass of students at UCC).

My goal was to learn as much about the person in front of me as possible, and try to add value to their life by taking a genuine interest in it. But still, even with the success I had at developing relationships, I was obsessed with the fact that no one was reaching out to me from home. *What had I done to deserve this?* I felt like I had fostered plenty of relationships and created friendships that would last a lifetime. Looking back, maybe I should've gotten off my high horse and reached out first. Obviously, I wasn't yet a believer in the law of reciprocity.

Then something magical happened; I received a message from Charles himself. Except it was from a platform that was out of my norm. He didn't use Facebook, email or even text- but a magical tool called LinkedIn. I rarely used the platform, but was ecstatic to see what he had written. He was angry at me too, but mentioned how I was missed by the house, football and rugby teams and the general student population.

Then something clicked inside me. *Why in the hell were we both irritated at one another?* We had both abandoned the initial reason why we had connected as friends. A deep empathy for others and the willingness to take the first step was what created our bond in the first place. Such hypocrites were we – and, looking back on the situation, I had known it deep down inside my frustrations. So, I took the next step and invited him to do a Skype call, so that we could catch up.

He readily agreed, creating a dynamic where we could go back to doing what we do best together. On the call, we laughed, shared our experiences and reminisced about prior days. It sparked something in the both of us that is now focal in our lives. We started communicating regularly from a distance. Whether it was short or long messages, it didn't matter. What did matter was the fact that we once again took a sincere interest in the other's life, which was helped along by the platform we were using. It was a place where he and I were building a brand between ourselves. We could see the benefits to establishing our personal brand on LinkedIn. It indirectly helped made me take the leap and come back to Canada. I decided to attend the Smith School of Business where, not-coincidentally, Charlie was starting in the fall.

By using our virtual relationship as a case study, we were able to implement steps that helped friends re-establish lapsed relationships across the continent. Simply put, friends love seeing, talking and knowing what is going on with someone's life. By utilizing different webinar groups and online-file-sharing applications, we were able to strengthen the connection between UCC boys. We first used relationships and word of mouth to share the phenomena with people. Now, we take advantage of our ever-growing presence to capture new opportunities for ourselves and friends. We have decided to create a company that helps job candidates differentiate themselves via video resumes, LinkedIn social selling, resume consulting and interview prepping. Through one of our relationships, we were able to gain a partnership with Onyx, an affordable option for tailor-made suits. Now we can help our clients feel confident about landing a job, knowing they have done everything possible, including looking great in a new suit.

Relationships, virtual and in-person, were the catalyst for our project. We've actually found that some virtual relationships have sprung up and surpassed their in-person counterparts, perhaps due to the differences in distance. An intentional relationship can be stronger than one created by proximity, such as a school or work setting. Regardless of the method of creation of a friendship, to be truly invested and interested in another person's life is by far the easiest, fastest and best way to foster relationships.

He Said: Charlie's Tale

What do a real estate agent, mortgage broker, family doctor, financial planner, salesperson, esthetician, public relations specialist, and business development specialist have in common? Each of their individual careers lives and thrives from the relationships that they have forged and fostered throughout their professional lives.

Whether you're fighting tooth and nail to climb the corporate ladder, or you're already sitting at the top, the key to success in business is in your relationships.

Don't get me wrong, relationships aren't the single defining factor that will make or break a career, but as author John C. Maxwell once said, *"Your network is your net worth."* This quote has always resonated with me, but I don't think that I understood the true meaning behind the clever play on words until I finished my first year of university studying in Canada at the Queen's Smith School of Business.

The harsh reality for myself, and students all over the world, is that summer jobs and internships are in high demand, but limited in number. Despite a surplus of talented candidates, corporations only have so much room for inexperienced professionals trying to get their foot in the door. I quickly came to this realization after being denied multiple job opportunities in a wide variety of fields. After realizing this, I began conducting a social study targeting older students to try to identify how they managed to secure their past summer jobs. I quickly came to notice a pattern – it's all about who you know. This is when I began to understand the power and potential of networking.

From the classrooms, to the world far beyond those concrete walls and paneled ceilings, there is one thing that brings people together...relationships. After reflecting on my own life over the past several years, What I've come to realize is that the seemingly small interactions that we have on a daily basis with one another shape our mannerisms and influence the outlook that we have on the world. The truth is that each and every one of the relationships that we cultivate helps us grow in a different way. We learn things from one another and teach those around us more than we could ever realize. This is the exact reason that I believe relationships are the focal point of business.

Looking back, I've had many influential friendships that I am proud to say have shaped me for the better. However, there is one specific relationship that stands out to me and, I believe that it has changed my outlook on the world and business for the better. My friendship with Jeff began all the way back in 8th grade, and has carried forward to this day.

In 2012, Jeff was a transfer student who began his journey alongside me at Upper Canada College, an all-boys high school located in Toronto, Ontario. Jeff is a year older than me, however being in separate grades never seemed to influence our strong relationship. After Jeff and I met for the first time, we quickly came to realize how much we had in common. We both skied at the same ski club, we both loved rugby and football, and most importantly we both loved people. From the get-go, I could see that Jeff had an innate ability to be personable. Rest assured, the ability to be personable is not a skill that everyone has, but it certainly is a quality that everyone appreciates. It's for this reason that I appreciated my friendship with Jeffrey so much. Jeff and I have quite similar mindsets and that is what has made it so easy to get along over the years.

Upper Canada College is a school that is rich with tradition. Separating students evenly into ten houses is one tradition that has carried forward through the years since its founding.

The administration does this to allow for friendly intramural sport competitions and mentorship opportunities. In Jeff's final year at Upper Canada College, he was elected the leader of our house by the student body. He had the opportunity to mentor the 80 young boys of Howard House. This is when Jeff and I really began to grow close as friends. It was our first experience working alongside each other as senior members of the house. After Jeff graduated and moved on to the next chapter in his life, I continued his leadership legacy and was elected one of the four prefect leaders of Howard's house. Mentoring was a big responsibility, but it allowed me to represent the house and become a role model for the younger grades, bridging the gap between the younger and older students.

After Jeff's graduation, we began to lose contact. I was still at our high school, and Jeff left Canada to attend university in California. Six months later our friendship was quickly revived when Jeff and I reconnected over LinkedIn. We began sending messages back and forth, and eventually scheduled a phone call where our relationship really came back to life. Jeff and I stayed in very good contact after that call. We talked throughout the duration of the school year and upon my graduation from Upper Canada College, I was delightfully surprised with the news that Jeff had decided to leave USC. He was going to continue his post-secondary education at the Queen's Smith School of Business alongside me in the class of 2020.

Throughout the school year, Jeff and I spent a lot of time together. We both shared a similar outlook on life and believed that one of the most valuable things gained from a university experience is the ability to meet and surround yourself with like-minded people. Jeff and I came to understand this more and more throughout the year, and eventually dedicated that next summer to meeting and connecting with like-minded individuals through a platform called LinkedIn.

When summer came around, I took a job working for a start-up company, where my role was to help find work for local freelancers in the area. In my spare time, I dedicated myself to fostering new relationships and meeting new people. By the end of the summer I had been able to help hundreds of freelancers begin to better market their skills and find work, something I had struggled with severely in my job application process only a few months prior.

Since then, Jeff and I have decided to live together and have become closer than ever, helping us make the decision to launch a business together. Now the two of us run a career preparation company that teaches students how to effectively market their skills and abilities to employers and find work with their dream companies. To this day, Jeff and I have made the focus of our business to meet and help as many new faces as we possibly can. After all, the people around us are the reason we are where we are today.

194

* * * * *

Twenty Comes Before Thirty

Randall C. Daniels

"This position has unlimited earning potential!"

Have you ever heard that in a job interview? Did you believe it?

Once you started working there, did you discover that even they didn't buy into their own hype? At least not using the approved sales methods that they've always used...

Well, allow me to share my story with you. I was an experienced sales rep, very accustomed to earning an annual six-figure income. I was transitioning into a new industry, by accepting my one-and-only job as an automobile sales rep. I took this job with anticipation of breaking records, competing nationally against the best sales reps and earning an "unlimited" six-figure income.

But my story doesn't start there; let me tell you how this journey began.

Like many children, I grew up outside, active and enjoyed playing sports. As time went on, I realized I had developed a love and passion to not only play, but to WIN! I became obsessed with being one of the best athletes in the park. I put in countless hours practicing and glancing at books to develop my skills. I was blessed to become a winner, playing the sports that I loved. Coaches would say to me, *"You could be special,"* but I didn't know what that really meant. I loved playing with older players because it made me better.

And yet, when I was asked as a child, *"What would you like to do when you grow up?"* my dreams were frowned upon. If I answered that I want to be a professional athlete, I received advice from so many mediocre experts that preached on the importance of striving for mediocrity.

Most didn't know any better: teachers, parents, relatives, and counselors in the area where I grew up. Everyone seemed to preach a common theme. If you want success in this world you need to get a college degree. That's the way it's always been. That's your ticket to a nice home with a white picket fence and a nice nest egg at retirement.

As I watched these mediocre experts grow old in my neighborhood, they again shared a common theme. Most lived check to check with no white picket fence and no more dreams of traveling the world at retirement. Most of them never even cracked an annual salary of $50,000 with their respective college degree. They were safely mediocre. Why was that the model they felt everyone should follow?

I'm so thankful I took the path less traveled. I was fortunate enough to travel throughout Europe playing basketball and boxing. The competitive drive and work ethic I developed from sports is precisely what fuels my determination for success today.

When I got my first sales job in the mall as a teenager, they gave me some training videos to watch. The videos resembled my little league coaches and their stress of training fundamentals. I believed in the videos the way I believed in my coaches. So, I watched the videos with fine detail. I had been hired as a porter, but I would usually get the stock put away long before my shift ended. So, one day the store manager asked me if I would like to come on the sales floor after putting away stock. I quickly observed that the seasoned sales reps were not utilizing many of the fundamentals taught in the videos. They thought it was better to do things the way they had always done them. What I learned as a teenage sales rep was that sports and sales have many similarities. The more fundamentally sound you are, the greater potential for success you have. I went on to have great success there and often outshined the more seasoned reps. Before graduating high school that company offered me a position as a manager.

Before I became a six-figure earner, I was working hard to earn $30,000 yearly. Other people were dictating my income. Because I didn't have a college degree, I only applied for jobs others said I would qualify for. When I interviewed at the company that would change my mindset forever, I neglected to go my 2nd interview. There were people younger than me working there making more than $120,000 yearly. I had a $30,000 mindset. I didn't think I was the right person for that job, because I hadn't acquired a college degree. That's the way it had always been done.

Fortunately for me, the sales manager of that company saw something in me that I didn't see in myself. He saw the swagger, the confidence and he understood life was about opportunities. He believed that if he gave me the opportunity, I possessed the other intangible qualities needed for great success. He called me and started selling me on why I should work for their company. Remember, I had ditched the 2nd interview!

Of course, I accepted the job and found that my strong work ethic, along with my fundamentally sound approach to sales would have a huge impact. I started breaking records on the wall, and made $75,000 my first year there – just in the last 10 months of that year. The astonishing part was this was the easiest job I had in my entire life. My income increased from $30,000 to $75,000 in short order, but more importantly, that position changed my mindset for life!

Your success doesn't depend on a college degree, it depends on you. Without a college degree, I got hired as the director of business development for Thomas More College. I competed for this position against many degreed applicants, so how did I get the job? My mindset was now different. I had tremendous confidence in my abilities because of my sports success, my work ethic, and my previous sales accomplishments. I saw the requirements for the job and I knew I had the ability to be successful. I had always been a fast starter and a quick learner. I believe enthusiasm should show in my work, so I pack my enthusiasm with me every day. I respond well to challenges and enjoy the opportunity to reap the rewards of hard work and dedication. I compete against myself daily to improve upon facets of my life and strive to be the best person I can. IT'S ALL ABOUT WHAT YOU BRING TO THE TABLE! I believe many of the professionals I interacted with assumed I had a degree of some type.

In 2003, while at the college, I founded and helped champion an organization called the Regional Association for Adult Higher Education. It is a consortium of regionally accredited colleges and universities in the Cincinnati and Northern Kentucky area. As the president of this organization, it was my job to convince these institutions of higher learning to work more closely with local businesses. We provided educational seminars, lunch and learn events and education fairs for corporations and small businesses. The education fairs and seminars help educate both employers and employees about new educational opportunities for working adults. The organization is still making a huge impact on our labor force today.

I have a resume full of successful sales jobs, but decided to get into auto sales because a dear friend suggested that I would have tremendous success with it. So, I decided to learn a new way of helping people and joined my friend at the dealership. While going through training, the general manager (GM) suggested I reach out to our top Cincinnati sales rep and pick his brain to glean some insight on how he sells 25 cars a month.

Before I contacted him, I looked up the sales stats on him and the other top sales reps nationwide. I discovered our top Cincinnati rep was #5 nationally. Not a bad brain to pick, but the #1 and #2 reps weren't in Cincinnati, they were both in Atlanta, Georgia. After this discovery, I wanted to call the reps in Atlanta because they both sold over 30 cars every month. Then I asked the GM, "Why would you tell me just to talk with the #5 rep, instead of the person who is consistently #1?"

His answer to me was that the Atlanta market was larger, and therefore the reason sales reps there were selling over 30 cars a month. He said, "Our market won't support sales like that, so 20-25 sales per month would be outstanding."

That's the way it's always been.

So, what did I do? I called the people who were our top 2 sales reps in the nation. The ones in Atlanta. They were both relatively tight-lipped and didn't share any golden nuggets or magical formula. They did share just a bit, and the thing they had in common that did stand out was hard work. If hard work was the secret sauce to 30+ cars per month, that was right up my alley. No stranger to hard work, I believed I was on the right path to compete for the top national sales spots. My mindset was not tainted by geographic location. Sports had given me the attitude and confidence that if they could do it, so could I.

I began to learn the system for selling cars at this dealership. The sales reps had to make a lot of outbound calls to generate leads. They wanted us to make over 50 calls per day even though we had a referral program.

That's the way it's always been.

I figured out a marketing strategy to dive deeper into our referral program. I approached my GM and our corporate office about my referral strategy ideas and got the approvals I needed. I was able to convince them to allow me to try my new approach by sharing some prior successes. After all, I had designed marketing material for myself and previous employers.

Now every day at work instead of dialing, dialing, dialing, I spent my time designing materials for my new marketing strategies. My marketing designs took a little while to create, but I had the know-how to design and to use them. Other sales reps would walk by my desk and say, "You need to get off that computer and get on that phone."

While I was unsure how it would ultimately play out, I just put my head down and plowed forward. I was determined to make my phone ring instead of making 50+ daily calls disturbing other people. None of the sales reps truly embraced the 50-call goal, and most reps struggled to accomplish that daily requirement. It was a relief not making surprise calls to disturb people who may no longer be in the market for a car. I was so determined to prove my strategy would work, I never had any desire to stop what I was doing and do it their way - the way it's always been.

Midway through the next month, I was among the top of the national leader board with 12 sales. I was most excited about the last 8 of my 12 sales, which happened during the week when my marketing plan was fully kicked in. That showed me the potential of selling 8 cars in a week. During my next weekly sales meeting, I said "I'm going to sell 30 cars this month."

One of the reps, who struggled to even sell 12 cars a month - the minimum to keep your job - really inspired me that day. He chuckled and said, "You have to sell 20 cars first."

When I sold my 20th car, I was able to smile and reply, "20 comes before 30."

I went on to sell 32 cars that month, and calls from our corporate office started coming in wondering how I did it. Everyone at our dealership just quietly observed my different approach, and I imagine they wondered if it was a fluke, or what kind of success I would have. As my success continued, other sales reps started asking for my help and input. Most of them were struggling to sell 15 cars and wanted to find out why my system worked. Some of the reps decided not to try my system because it required work and dedication. Some tried for a bit, and stopped for the very same reasons. They went back to the way it's always been.

I went on to average 30 car sales per month during my career there. I broke and currently hold almost every company record in the Cincinnati market. I was always the top seller in Cincinnati, but I never finished #1 nationally. However, I am the only sales rep that can boast finishing nationally in the top five every year during my time there. My results caught someone's attention, because this $800 million company began duplicating my marketing efforts and still do to this day. It's the new way it's always been.

Eventually I moved on to bigger and better things for my children. Having 8 children, I spent many hours at youth sporting events and church events and I loved every minute. They were active in so many different things and I needed to be there to cheer for and support them. I began doing sales coaching and training to gain more control of my time. I had already been running many of the sales trainings at the dealership, so this was a natural fit for me. That dealership became one of my clients for many years.

I still love the game of basketball and I get tremendous pleasure in sharing the knowledge I learned with young people. I spend hours in the gym every week and train athletes of all ages from basic fitness to basketball skills. I have a goal to one day sponsor an organization that helps seniors and

202

everyone become athletes for life. Even if all they can do is just simple walking, they'll be recognized as athletes.

I've had the availability to help others because of my sales background and ability to think outside-the-box. It has afforded me the opportunity to have a little more control of my time while working. Fostering new thinking with an objective mind-set can transform busyness into actual productiveness. Learn to work more brilliantly by identifying the best use of your time and talent. You can have dramatic improvement in productivity with minor improvement in skills, and more time to do the things you love to do.

Don't allow others to cap your potential because of the way it's always been.

Never Satisfied

Devamalya De

My boss handed me the promotion letter: I had just been promoted to a senior manager position and also got a sixty per cent increment. His next question: "Was I Happy? Satisfied?"

I remember I wasn't able to force a smile - my mind was racing. I had done the calculations over and over again; and arrived at an eighty per cent hike as the bare minimum I needed to avail a mortgage loan for an apartment in the Mumbai suburbs. Now with a scaled down increment, the loan and the house had to wait. May be one year, may be more...This was eight years ago.

I had graduated from college five years prior, and with a sufficient academic record got a decent campus placement. But one year into my first job, I was on the lookout for a bigger and better deal. As a civil engineer from one of India's prestigious universities with a post graduate in construction management, I felt corporate life should be a cakewalk, with companies ready to open up their purse strings to get me on board. I even received offers from some companies abroad, but felt their package wasn't good enough and left them on the table.

Job and money satisfaction seemed to elude me. Friends and relationships did as well. I lived the life of a recluse, with just occasional contact with my sister who lived in the same area of the city. This seclusion extended to my office. It seemed I was always ready to put colleagues to the sword who strayed outside of the company rules and regulations. My boss watched everything in silence. Then one day he told me: "If you continue like this, you will never be successful. In a field like construction, contact points are many, and you don't get anywhere by pissing people off."

That was my first wake-up call.

And then there was the second call. It so happened that my company was bidding for a project in another state and in order to submit a competitive quote, it was imperative that we get the local rates of materials and labour. I had batchmates from my graduate school classes who were working in all corners of the country and the globe. But here was I, living in a silo: a self-centred, moribund existence and not wanting to reach out to my own friends and batchmates. Deep down a voice asked me: *How can you reach out to your batchmates when you are still not a Manager !?*

With such a deep-seated and yet superficial prejudice, I lived life as a loner. How could I interact with those who had graduated with me before I become 'something'? It was a benchmark set internally by my psyche - a mental block.

Then one day my boss summoned me and asked if I had been able to find the local rates for the out-of-state project. I kept quiet, with my face down, clearly revealing I hadn't. He continued: "You don't get rates on the Internet; for that you have to do some environment study; reach out to your network, to your contacts, friends and batchmates."

That opened my eyes. That day for the first time, I opened up to my friends and batchmates about the help I required, and was immediately inundated with help in all possible ways. I realized the importance of asking for help. It doesn't make one small, it only endears one to other people who notice your vulnerability and pitch in with whatever they can.

Around the same time, I was also looking to get settled; I was looking for a good match of a girl. I remember there were a few I would begin to get to know, but as soon as I realized their shortcomings, I would back away from any relationship. This continued for months and years. Finally, a colleague and a dear friend of mine told me: "Why do you judge people so much? Just get to know them, and get excited by the differences. If you both enjoy each other's differences over time, it means you can settle down as man and wife."

I applied the learnings from my colleague and friend, and within a year's time I was married.

Fast forward by four years; I am now married and blessed with an angel (a son). We went out on a short trip out of Mumbai to a beach resort to de-stress and recharge my batteries. I could not enjoy it. Here was I, staying at a five-star property, with the best company in tow, looking out at the aquamarine waters of the beach - but my mind was again racing. *Oh, the good times will pass away in a jiffy,* I thought. *Soon I will have to return to the grind.*

As I look back on those formative years when I was young, I remember I was never satisfied. If I have to analyze and break down the reasons, there were several.

> I planned too much and fixated myself on those plans. I never had a back-up plan in place.

> I never lived in the moment; I was always thinking of the next – job, vacation and so on.

> If I ever met new people, I would subconsciously scour for what they had to offer me and not the other way round.

> I tended to judge people.

The series of interactions with my boss and colleague, set me up to break away from the rigid cobwebs in my mind, from the deep-seated prejudices which had held me back.

As life opened up to me in its myriad hues and colours over time, I made a point to face it head-on with the following remedial measures in how I responded to life.

I never stopped planning, but knew plans were meant to fail 90% of the time. I started having plans B, C and so on. (*The most remarkable things in life happen when we have least planned for them!*)

I consciously set myself up to be aware: awareness is all about being alive. (*It's neither our dreams nor what happens to us in life which are real, but it's our awareness.*)

I started meeting, interacting and knowing people without any selfish interest, but to connect at a deeper psychological level: not with a motive to receive but with a heart to give

I stopped judging people completely – this helped me bond with them and make great connections and deep friendships. (*When you stop judging people, you start loving them.*)

If I have to reflect, my professional life - interactions with my boss and colleagues - helped shape my orientation towards life to understand, relish and cherish the Wealth of Satisfaction in the true sense of the term.

The realization that runs deep down is that bounty and plenty don't lead us to satisfaction in life: it has more to do with being aware, going with the flow that life is, being flexible, having deep relationships sans selfish interests, and loving people without judging them. I can hardly be called rich among my peers from college. but I do have a lot of things which money can't buy. And those count.

We are but a speck of stardust and we will return to the dust one day. Satisfaction is not a destination, it's here and now; if only we live life in the moment, by being aware, unselfish and in love with one another!

* * * * *

A Walk in My Shoes

Angie Grimes

We are all searching for the same thing in this life; at our core, we all want success and acceptance. There is very little that we search for that does not fall under those two umbrellas. I know that personal success has always been a driving factor for me.

Keep in mind that success and acceptance can look very different to each individual. We all have our own version of what a "successful" person does, says and projects. We all know what "acceptance" feels like, and without a doubt we can all envision what this means to us.

My version of success has changed considerably over time. When I was first starting my career, success was financial reward and gain. My parents were very young when they had me and I grew up in a single wide trailer. As I progressed through life I took the less traveled path, I did not actually graduate high school. You see, I experienced a considerable amount of family issues which led me to leave home and get married at 16. Yes, you read that right; I was married at 16 years old.

The first question I always get when sharing this part of my life is, "Did you get pregnant?" (The answer is no). The second question is *"How?"*, but I really think the more important question should be *"Why?"* My parents got divorced when I was 6 and I bounced back and forth between vastly different households. My mom suffers from mental illness and there were many days that my life did not project a "normal" routine. There are many things that we are exposed to as children that we don't have control over and don't understand, but typically these are where our beliefs are formed.

I was able to use my environment as I was growing up as a catalyst for what I did not want in my life. So, I knew that I wanted more in my life and I developed the belief that I could achieve success if I worked hard. Although I experienced success in my career efforts, in the back of my mind I felt that I had to work harder than most to make up for my lack of schooling. This propelled my obsession with the next achievement, I began living mostly in the future of what could be. It is where I thought I felt most "whole." I knew that if I continued to pursue my path to what my version of a successful person was, I would have everything that I ever desired. And in truth, it worked, but only for a while.

I experienced an incredibly varied career path from medical billing, to accounting, to being a paralegal and even web development. I was constantly looking for the next best thing, so I could learn more and achieve more (aka make more).

Let's go back to 2002 – I was fortunate enough to co-found my first business. It was my first brush with entrepreneurship and I was hooked. It was varied enough to keep my attention and I was an inherent problem solver, so being an entrepreneur really aligned with how I was structured.

We began this business initially on eBay selling used shoes that my partner sourced from swap meets. Our first purchase was for 30 pair of used shoes and we sold through 28 pair with a 400% profit margin. SHOEBACCA.com was born and within two years we ramped up to just over $5M in sales and continued to grow steadily year after year.

In the process, I had become a workaholic. I was in a thriving career making millions – for others. I had co-founded a company and had title and authority, but was very naïve in the way of business and had made a partnership deal that did not allow for my personal success. I'll chalk this up to the school of hard knocks.

I was furiously checking huge accomplishments off my list. Then there came a point that I began to struggle meeting those continued accomplishments. I was overwhelmed, stretched way too thin and feeling that the house of cards I had built for myself could collapse at any moment.

Looking back, I was playing a dangerous game with myself. I had actually let my success and failure with my career define who I was as a person. Who I was became tied to how much I could accomplish. When my accomplishments became fewer and farther between and ultimately stalled, I equated that to my self-worth and I began to spiral.

I used to be the type of person that would dig in and say: *You can do this, you can do anything!* I would just push harder to try to make it happen. I was of the mindset that if I could control more of what was happening with the business I could get it, and myself, back on track. The reality unfolded that in trying to control more, not only was I putting my health at risk, I was stifling my business. My staff could feel the pressure that I was putting on myself and, by extension, them. Although, I did not even recognize it at the time, I was not allowing them the freedom to help grow the business. I was handcuffing them to do it my way, period.

Ultimately, I was pushed out of the business and it crushed me personally. I had more blood, sweat, tears and time invested in that business than I care to recount. I had hired and developed a wonderful team. I ultimately let them down by not allowing them to collectively grow. I came to the sad realization that I had allowed my business to outgrow me.

With this experience I felt battered, defeated and really lost. I had allowed myself to become a reflection of my work, and who was I without my work? It took time for me to recover, but I began to realize that SHOEBACCA is a success story. As

President and COO I helped lead 170 people as we diversified and sold through multiple channels, including our own.

I experienced a shift in my perception, not only about who I was but about what I had accomplished over the decade that I led that organization. My achievements were vast and grand. Are there situations that I would have handled differently? Without a doubt. But I did the best I could with what I had in the moment.

The process of self-discovery taught me the importance of compassion for myself, and this led me to recognize the compassion that I have for others. We are all comprised of our moments in time and the raw vulnerable truth is that we all do the best with what we have in the moment. I really want you to take some time to let that one to sink in...You did the best you could with what you had in the moment; no regrets.

We think we are incredibly different from one another, but we all go through similar experiences. My hope is that you can relate to some of this and recognize the beauty of the adversity that we all face. Accept your successes and failures, knowing that all of those experiences shaped the incredibly unique person that makes up who you are today. Find some compassion for yourself and for others.

Football, Orange Groves and the Business of Inventing

Don Skaggs

In the early startup days of one of my companies, I was struggling with challenges that felt like I was pressed against crushing odds. This was at a time very early in my career, and one of the things I did not know yet was that this was typical at the beginning stages of almost any startup, project or endeavor of significance.

I was working with my dad in a new business where we faced many challenges as we developed new technologies and launched new products into a market that had some very large competitors. I had the opportunity in those days of living on both sides of the fence: marketing and sales, as well as research and development. This meant that I not only had the opportunity to interact with customers and learn what their painful problems were, but I also worked in the creative, "what-if" part of discovery to find new solutions to those problems. I learned early on that while wearing a lot of hats is a necessary element of many startups, it can still feel like a daunting and overwhelming part of business. As the new challenges of turning our ideas into a real, tangible business mounted, the pressures were starting to take their toll. Competitors were starting to sit up and take notice of us, and the fear of competing with a large company was becoming all too real. I was starting to believe that those giant competitors we were facing were just going to grind us underfoot.

It was then that Dad, seeing the frustration I was experiencing, told me this story from his football days. He had played for a high school in a small eastern Kentucky town in the 1950's, and while I heard a lot of his football stories growing up, this was something new. It turned out to be a good thing, because hearing it for the first time at that moment really impacted my career and life.

Dad had become something of a football legend in his hometown. Decades later when he returned for a reunion, one elderly gentleman told him that the most exciting football he had ever watched, professional, college or otherwise, was when he watched Dad on the field in high school. My dad had made Kentucky All-Star, and had earned nicknames such as "greased lightning". But such was not always so.

When he first made the team, Dad spent most of his first season on the bench. The coach, as well as many other people around him, thought he just didn't have the natural build and bulk to be competitive on the field. *Those other boys will break your legs*, was typical of the jaunts he would hear.

However, during the summer months, he implemented a plan that would change things dramatically. You see, my grandfather owned orange groves down in Florida, and would take the family down there each summer, tending to the groves. During those summers in a 1950's Florida, you would have found my dad in those orange groves, and it would have been a peculiar sight. You would have seen a teenage boy running all-out, directly at an orange tree. Just before making contact, he would cut and change direction, moving to the left or the right of the tree. He practiced this over, and over, and over again, until he developed the skill of accelerating on the cut. In the telling of this story, Dad said that he got to the point where he could feel the edges of the leaves on the trees brushing the sides of his arms on the cut.

The next fall arrived, school began, and with it the start of football season. There came a day that my dad was finally put onto the field, and what happened next became football history for that high school. When he intercepted a pass, he held onto the ball and headed toward the end zone. He ran all-out, directly at the opposing team's players. These were boys of mammoth stature and frame compared to my dad, all meaning to mow him down in short order. To their utter shock and surprise, he ran right at them and then cut away, accelerating on the cut. Just as with the leaves in the orange groves, he felt the edges of their fingers brushing his arms as they reached out for him. He did this again and again, rushing his way to the goal and making a winning touchdown.

He did not possess the size and strength of those he was going toe-to-toe with. So, what was it that gave my dad the ability to win over those literally crushing odds?

Desire, creativity and persistence.

Spending those summers in Florida, he could have just sat and worried about the next season, or become despondent and just quit. But he wanted to *play football.*

He could have continued to practice the conventional way; he could have done the same things his opponents and teammates were doing to get better. Had he continued to compete by using the same procedures, he would have most likely failed. Instead he thought about what he had or could do that the others did not. What he came up with was something no one else was doing, something that he could do, and something that would even the playing field for him.

And then he practiced. He was not born with this talent. If he had only thought about doing it, he would have failed. If he had only practiced when he felt like it, or not had practiced enough, he would have failed. But he did practice, again and again, and then again. He practiced until he could feel the edges of the leaves just barely brushing his upper arms knowing that the same would be true with the enormous linebackers coming at him out on the field.

Dad's timing in relating this story to me, as his timing back then on the football field, was perfect. This was the vision I needed to overcome my current obstacles and adopt a strategy of seeing the bigger picture. I needed to develop my own creative plan to put into practice - the kind that can pit a little David against a towering Goliath and win. Win in spite of "how things are supposed to be," or what is generally accepted as conventional wisdom. This new perspective made a profound difference in how I approached and dealt with new problems both in my business and in life. It's amazing how the problems themselves seemed to somehow almost mystically change. What once felt hopeless was now solvable, stumbling-blocks turned into stepping-stones, and problems became opportunities to do something everyone else thought was impossible.

I think this story of a young high school football player all those years ago can teach some important life lessons. We can feel like we are facing crushing odds in most every part of our day. Problems, like those mammoth linebackers, can seem a lot bigger than we are when coming at us. We don't have enough resources. We don't have enough time. We don't have a lot of the things we think we need. If we focus on what we don't have, it becomes overwhelming, disheartening and creates a spirit of failure within us. If we allow this feeling to overtake us and drive our decisions, it can kill our desire. It can propel us to eventual failure in business and in life, many times being ultimately caused by our very own unrealized choices and actions.

But if we have the desire, if we decide – on purpose – that what we want is more important than "How things are supposed to be," we can move forward. We can do things that others are not doing, find abilities we didn't know we had, and implement strategies we just haven't yet thought of. And these types of actions in this new and different direction can become a game-changer for us.

Get creative. Dad knew he had to do something no one else was. Use those hidden creative abilities that you already possess to come up with new ways to do things. Focus on what you can do, instead of what you can't. Once you begin to implement that plan, something mystical begins to happen. You will see that you've given yourself that needed edge to overcome the challenges or the present adversity you are facing, and they are no longer overwhelming you. This realization can be very empowering, and help to give you the momentum to move forward in other areas that before seemed impossible.

Persist. Dad didn't get better at football by just thinking about running at trees in that Florida orange grove. Instead, he tested his creative plan and turned it into something real. Every day during that hot summer in Florida, while others were at the beach or sunning themselves by the pool, Dad was in the orange groves, likely looking ridiculous. First, it was just an idea. The doing of it made it real. The practice made it effective.

If there is a skill necessary to implement your idea, find out what it is, learn how to do it, and then practice it over, and over, and over again. And then practice it some more. Practice can be unbelievably empowering. Once you become skilled at something, you own it. Those big boys coming at you can't break your legs if they reach out and can only brush your upper arms with the edges of their fingers. And you can't fear them if you know that.

This was just one example of the many great lessons Dad taught me, lessons that have served me well and ones that I have strived to share with others in order to pay it forward. In the years since I learned these important truths they have carried me through a lot of the tough times. I believe that living these types of lessons has helped in the ultimate success I have had in business and in life.

My Dad once told me that he could take everything that he gained by playing football, add a dollar and it would buy him a cup of coffee. I beg to differ.

My Unseen Truth

Eartha Watts-Hicks

Many of us are battling a health issue; struggling through treatment, hoping for a cure, reaching for a plateau where our condition is in remission or, at the very least, is under control. Those of us who are, know battling an ailment can be taxing, not only physically, but emotionally.

In December of 2005, I awoke in the middle of the night and everything was black. Even after I allowed my eyes to adjust to dim lighting, all I saw were shapes outlined in florescent colors—pinks, yellows, greens, and blues. I didn't panic. I assumed that I was overtired and went back to sleep. The next morning, I could see again, but when I looked in the mirror I noticed the whites of my eyes were red. Assuming this was conjunctivitis (pink-eye), I scheduled an appointment with my physician. I thought it wise, since around this same time, I was walking around with this random pain in my side. When I made it to my doctor visit, my main concern was the pain I was experiencing in the kidney area. My doctor scheduled me for a CAT scan, but was more concerned with my eyes. Once he examined them, he did not prescribe the drops for pink-eye as I expected, but immediately referred me to an eye specialist. The eye specialist then referred me to another specialist. After roughly three months of keeping up with one appointment after another, I was ultimately diagnosed with bilateral Uveitis.

Uveitis is an inflammation that occurs inside the eye, affecting the uvea. Or as my Uveitis specialist explained to me, my white blood cells were attacking the insides of both my eyes, causing damage to my own eye tissue. This rare condition is not contagious but can be caused by several factors, among them, parasitic infection and Sarcoidosis. My CAT scan results revealed various complications throughout my lungs, kidneys, liver, and gallbladder, all benign tumors. Receiving these results, my Uveitis specialist immediately pinpointed Sarcoid as the cause. From his experience that was the one condition likely to affect the eyes, liver, and other organs. After blood work and a full workup of STD testing came back as inconclusive, he recommended that I get a chest x-ray. By this point I was fed up with these tests, and the anguish that came along with worrying about more bad news at doctor's offices, so I put that off, delaying longer and longer. About a year passed, and it was ultimately my own primary care physician who scheduled the chest x-ray. Sure enough, I was diagnosed with Stage I Sarcoid. The Sarcoid, for the most part was asymptomatic. Dealing with Uveitis was another matter altogether.

Upon being diagnosed with bilateral Uveitis, I was initially only mildly concerned. My Uveitis specialist was young, practical, and confident. Right away, he had outlined a regimen for me. He said my odds for success were about 50/50, which I immediately shook off. He prescribed some steroid drops, and I began treatment, prayerfully optimistic. In my mind, especially because of my young doctor's confidence, Uveitis was as easily treated and cured as pink-eye. Considering them one and the same, I was sure that after a few drops and a few short weeks, this "problem" would be taken care of, and everything would return to normal. But then, somewhere around my second or third visit to my specialist, I encountered a fellow Uveitis patient in the waiting room, a woman around my age who had been battling this for eight years. I talked to this woman, and listened as she gave me her account of cortisone eye injections with a very long needle, subsequent cataract diagnosis, glaucoma, eye surgery, and vision loss. I immediately became depressed and felt that my own doctor had not fully explained the magnitude of the seriousness of this disorder.

After that, though the changes in my vision were gradual, for a while, my experience chronicled exactly what that other patient described. First, I saw tiny dark spots. These later expanded until they gave me the impression that a swarm of large bugs were flying at me. In Uveitis terms, these are known as "floaters." Then, in addition to this, my vision occluded with dark threads, first one, and then others, until it seemed as if I were viewing the world through a filthy screen. In Uveitis terms, this is known as "spider webs." Uveitis is a condition where white blood cells attack eye tissue, as if they were a foreign body or implanted, or simply did not belong as part of one's body system. This being the case, my vision was going through some changes. My eyes became extremely sensitive to light. I adapted by doing everything in the dark and wearing dark shades in the sunlight. For months at a time, no one around me could turn on bright lights, as that would cause me more eye pain. The pain was intense, a burning the equivalent of trying to recover from exposure to chlorine or sand, with one difference the pain was constant. My night vision diminished; I could no longer see beyond a few feet. Because this problem was occurring within the eyes, the changes in my vision could not be improved with corrective lenses. My doctor changed my prescription from the steroid drops to an immunosuppressant. I was in agony, but I did experience a brief reprieve. I was also given a software program known as EyeQ that was actually intended to teach speed reading. This program strengthened my eye muscles, and along with the medication, improved my vision. My Uveitis was controlled, and I was relieved. My vision seemed to be returning to normal.

But then, my health insurance provider refused to honor my prescription because it was not a generic drug. At the time, it was not available in any generic form and was also extremely expensive. Only one pill daily was required for my condition, but that one pill cost nearly $100. My doctor was now required to send in medical evidence proving that, for my condition, this medication was "medically necessary." I thank God that this young doctor was relentless about it. For the next two and a half weeks, my doctor, the pharmacy, and insurance company faxed paperwork back and forth and played phone tag. The matter was resolved after about three or four weeks, but by then my vision had deteriorated. According to my doctor, I experienced a 50% loss of vision. At one point, I was unable to read. My expression contorted to the point where I always appeared angry, but I was actually wincing from pain and squinting to try to see clearer. My doctor now had me on both the immunosuppressant and the steroid eye drops. Soon, I had circles on the corners of my eyes where the eye drops had bleached away pigment from my skin. I now wore sunglasses during the day and evening, even in the wintertime. I was also diagnosed with cataracts.

Meanwhile, I was still writing, but now had a renewed appreciation for everything I saw. Beauty was in dust, in clouds, in any and everything, and that love was transferred to the page when I wrote. For the most part, I remained quiet about my ordeal. My family knew, but I didn't even share what I was going through with some of my closest friends. Yet, I found myself preparing for the worst, instructing those who depended on me how to carry on in my absence. Even though I was praying for healing, I asked everyone I knew to pray for me, as if my own prayers weren't enough. It was as if instead of counting my blessings, part of me was actually counting down, and I was only allotted eight years. I put on weight, partly because of the steroid medication I was taking, but mainly due to seeking comfort in Häagen-Dazs chocolate chip cookie dough ice cream.

In the midst of this, my mother reminded me, "If you pray don't worry; if you worry don't pray." At some point, I don't remember when exactly, but the message sank in. I realized I had to make up my mind to either live in fear or live by faith. I had to stop believing what my own eyes were telling me and trust God. And even though this was a dark time in my life in more ways than one, I buckled down and focused on the positives. I had children to care for and the love and support of family and friends. God had brought me through so many trials in the past, "No weapons formed against me shall prosper!" Surely, He wouldn't leave me now. "All power is of God Creator of Heaven and Earth."

Then, at the insistence of my neighbor, I reached out. I asked a pastor we knew to pray for me. He did, and explained that by my faith I would be healed. He told me at my next doctor's visit, my doctor wouldn't find anything wrong. I sensed God's presence in that moment, and I believed I would be healed. Sure enough, my next visit, my doctor saw no trace of the cataracts, no sign of inflammation, and he remarked how my eyes "never looked better." God heals.

Today, thank God, my Uveitis is controlled. My vision is great. But as a result of the experience, I can relate to those who are battling. Health battles are not just physical; they are also of the spirit. Depression does nothing but impede progress. If we expect the worst, more than likely we will not be disappointed. Instead, we should educate ourselves, with our objective being health and healing, disregard the gory stories, and focus on the positives. Although, we may be suffering, we must nevertheless, stay focused, follow through with treatment responsibly, and above all remain faithful. Even when we are faced with "facts," we need to trust God. Because, after all, the battle isn't ours; it's His.

This selection was first published in the COSIA.NET Cultivating Our Sisterhood International Association a

501(c)(3) nonprofit. It has also been included in Graffiti Mural, my self-published collection of poetry, flash fiction, and personal essays, released August 1, 2016.

Lessons from Little League

Scott Taylor

"Winning is not a sometime thing; it's an all the time thing. You don't win once in a while; you don't do things right once in a while; you do them right all of the time. Winning is a habit. Unfortunately, so is losing."

~ Vince Lombardi, Coach - Green Bay Packers

I was born the youngest of five children and influenced by their mistakes. My father had his back fused at an early age and never amounted to anything, living off disability. My mother worked 2-3 jobs at times to pay the bills. The best outlook we children had for success was to get a good labor job and live to the extent such a position could afford. This limit seemed formidable because we knew no other opportunities and couldn't afford college or further education. My older brothers got into drugs and mischief, and spent some time in jail. Observing this pattern, I decided I wanted something better. I am the first person ever in the history of my family to attend college, and did so with a scholarship, grants and student aid. Unfortunately, my degree only served me for 18 months, when I found I would never make enough money with it to care for a family.

My father was a simple yet strong man, and although he was not highly educated, he had an uncanny grasp of strategy. He loved to win at every game or sport and would use any level of stratagem, sophistry or even cheating to win. He once coached a little league baseball team and even there, he had to win. In one game, his team was winning by one point after the third inning. However, as the fourth inning proceeded, the umpire made a few bad calls, which caused the other team to take the lead. He was angered by this and called time out.

Contriving a rather clandestine strategy he called his team into a huddle, and told them under no circumstances were they to get another out; over throw the ball, drop it, do anything but get them out. The inning continued with the opposing team continually rounding the bases and leading by more than 20 points while they laughed my dad's team to scorn. Suddenly, my father's plan was fulfilled and he yelled out, "That's it! Game over! We win!"

As the umpire and the other coach gathered together and a few angry words were tossed around, my father returned to the team victorious. He had pulled out the rule book showing that all games will be played to six innings or 90 minutes, whichever came first. If the game is stopped at 90 minutes the score at the end of the last finished inning will be the final score for the game. He won.

Although I was intrigued and impressed by my father's ability to win at all costs, I also felt shame and embarrassment for him when it was obvious to everyone that he won by cheating. In my youth, I noticed the win more than the embarrassment, so I would also do anything to win. As I matured, I began to feel a win wasn't really a win when I cheated. This pricking of conscience became so engrained that I started to become nauseated and a little depressed whenever I even thought of a scheme or lie to win. My father's need to win was deeply rooted in my system but his unsavory tactics were quickly waning from my repertoire of strategies. Without the use of my father's tactics, winning came from hard work. Strategy was always a major part of winning but doing it honestly required learning, skill development, overcoming obstacles and dealing with hardships.

Being an entrepreneur is a hard and arduous endeavor especially when lacking a proper mentor. It often takes more time and effort and with less reward for your time than if you held a simple job. Nevertheless, after years of experience in sales and marketing, I had created my own consulting company. During the tenure of this endeavor, I had a severe accident on my motorcycle, which knocked me out, put a hole in my head, broke my clavicle and left me with road rash over much of my body. This caused me to lose a few accounts and, while healing, I was earning about 58 cents per hour over several months.

Finally, I picked up a project with an insurance agency who hired me to inspire their agents to sell more. Out of the 115 branches of the company across America, they were ranked 3rd and had been for a few years. They wanted to be number one. It was after I took the assignment that they informed me I must be licensed to sell insurance in order to train insurance agents. This added to the time I was without income and our situation was approaching dire. But I procured my license as instructed.

Then I discovered I needed to be actively selling insurance in order to maintain my license, so I started selling as well as training. I only worked part-time (3 days per week), because I had another client I was working with at this time. After two months, I was only earning about $800 per month, which barely covered my house payment. My wife was complaining and our savings were depleted. Quitting seemed like the most pragmatic thing to do.

However, if I was to inspire others I could hardly do so by quitting, and quitting was not in my nature unless the position went against my morals and ethics. Then the transmission fell out of my car and I had to get a new one, my mother made our house payment and everyone was telling me it was time to give it up because I was now "becoming a burden on my family." The stress was unbearable but I still couldn't quit.

It was during my third month that I found my groove. I stopped selling the way I was taught and followed my own instincts. Like my dad's methods, theirs was uncomfortable to me because it appeared to be a form of deception. You see, we were selling affordable insurance, which meant we didn't cover everything. As part of the sales training, I was taught not to tell people about things we didn't cover. That was a negative, and to sell more insurance we needed to keep it positive, then they emphasized again; we were not to discuss negative things.

The change I made during my third month was to be more honest through disclosure. I would tell people; "We are going to save you $600 per month in insurance premiums, but don't think that means you can go out and buy a new house or car. Take that money and put it into a medical savings account to cover those things we don't. We don't cover MRI's, so if you end up needing one, that will be $1500 out of your pocket. Now, if you never need an MRI or have any additional medical expenses, you will have a great retirement income."

This insurance was ideal for healthy people but not great for the unhealthy. If I walked into someone's home who was overweight and on oxygen, I would simply tell them there was far better coverage available for unhealthy people than this and walk away from the sale. To my surprise, they would stop me and ask for my card. They knew some healthy family members and friends they wanted me to meet because they appreciated my honesty.

When other agents' customers needed an MRI, and received a surprise bill because it wasn't covered, they dropped the insurance. When my customers needed one they said, "Scott warned us about this," took care of it themselves, and kept the insurance. During that third month I earned $3500, and soon after started making that much per week.

There were nearly 40 agents in that office and never at any time had I been the top salesperson at the end of the week.

However, at the end of the year the branch manager called me into his office to inform me that I was ranked one of the top 20 agents. I told him that hardly seemed like much of an achievement in an office of 40 people. He then smiled and said, "Not in our office, in the company. You are in the top 20 of over 5000 agents."

I looked at him dumbfounded and asked how that was possible when I was never even the top agent any week in this branch. He told me it was because my business stayed on the books. That is when I understood the value of sales built on my integrity. The real honor was when people started asking my advice. It was then I knew I made it and was finally respected.

Anyone who learns to love work and accomplishment will succeed at whatever they do in life and maybe even excel in a discipline they have never considered. If a sports junkie meat-head like myself can change his attitude, gain integrity, strategize my tactics and increase my willingness to learn from everyone, to turn myself into a winner, so can you. Make work a pleasure and winning a habit and you will always end up on top, regardless of your vocation. It's always a climb to make it to the top but if you're willing and tenacious about getting there, you will. They may slow you down but they can never stop you.

My greatest achievement has been my ability to succeed with my integrity intact. I believe that is what makes other people want to celebrate your successes. People recognize honesty, a willingness to sacrifice for others, and hard work. Once you have earned a good reputation, they are excited to help you succeed. Success should never be a lonely endeavor. Be that person, and have that attitude, and others will want to help you succeed. You'll get there faster if you take others with you. It's not just the money, but bringing others with you on the journey to success that produces the real joy in business.

* * * * *

Trek of Purpose

Raúl Socha

"...I have found a desire within myself that no experience in this world can satisfy; the most probable explanation is that I was made for another world...."

~ *C.S. Lewis*

Preface of a Trek

I have walked many paths, been many places and believed many things; I have searched and yearned for that thing called happiness and purpose in life. I have had moments of sorrow and moments of joy. I have experienced poverty, wealth, secular fun, and moments of power. I have found it is all meaningless if there is no purpose or legacy to leave after I am gone. I realized one day, there will be a time when I will die, and my soul will be in another place. I would rather it be heavenly, and filled with memories of contributions I have made to society. At one point in my life, that question charged directly into my path, and I had to make a decision: Where do I want my soul to be after my death? Where do I want to spend the rest of my life, eternally?

I have found that a life without a purpose is not worth living. I have discovered that my purpose is to walk with God; serve mankind in any areas I can with all my heart, soul and mind; be an excellent man, husband, father, son, colleague, servant, and leader. The trials and challenges of this world are a great opportunity for growth in all areas of life. I have been taken on a path of personal, academic, financial, and professional growth, to then be able to serve and fulfill my calling and have an impact in society and perhaps leave a legacy in this world.

Growing Up Made in Colombia: Start of a Trek.

My name is Raúl Socha. I am originally from Colombia, South America and experienced various circumstances in my youth: poverty, middle class, and with a mixture of wealth and some influence over other people. I experienced many good and bad things when I was a child, and the foundation of my childhood could be described in one word: love. Although my birth was not planned, and took my parents by surprise, they decided to embrace the daunting task of having a child at an early age.

Later in life, I learned that my parents had married mainly because I was on the way. They both probably felt obligated to raise me, and may not have known what marriage would entail. As a little child, I viewed my parents as great role models; my father worked hard to support us and my mother ran the chores of the house. When I was almost two years old, my mother gave birth to my brother, Alejandro.

I do not recall much about the early years, but I do remember that my brother and I were good friends and inseparable. We used to play with cars and had a strong relationship. I remember the first day of school when my brother came to me running for help. I did not really know what was happening, until a handful of kids came and surrounded us; my instinct told me that my brother had picked a fight and had come to me for help. After measuring all the options, I picked up my lunch box by the string, grabbed my brother and turned around in a circle, hitting every kid around us. Then I took my brother and ran to the first teacher I could find. This event taught me a couple of valuable lessons; first, that my brother would turn to me in times of trouble, and second, that I would not let him down whatever the circumstances. I have also helped him grow by sharing the lessons I have learned on my own journey.

We grew up in a small town called Fusagasuga, located west of the Capital (Bogota). As time went by, the relationship between my parents deteriorated; I believe this had a marked impact on my life. My father's business started to prosper and he did not spend as much time at home. My mother, in turn, became bitter and took part of her frustration and anger out on my brother and me. I then learned that my father had several affairs with other women and this was very devastating on my mother. I still have vivid images of her telling me not to do what my father did, that I should treat women with respect and honor them. When I had a girlfriend or a wife, I had to honor the relationship, and be there for them.

As my father's business continued to flourish, he just spent time working. His thrill was negotiating the buying and selling of cars, and his food business. He loved to make deals and became very shrewd at making profitable ones. His business scored accounts with several military agencies and things were good for several years. In his free time, my father enjoyed playing billiards and used to play with his friends at a club on the weekends. He became so passionate about it that he bought the club to learn more about the business. For many years I resented his habit of drinking too much alcohol. His habit of cheating on my mother also made me angry enough that I did not want to be my father's son. My mother had several nervous breakdowns because of the ongoing situation, and I just wanted to grow up quickly to take her far away from my father to protect her.

After several years, my sisters came into the family picture; Catalina, Ana Maria and Laura Daniela. After they were born, it seemed that my father had a change of heart and slowed down on the drinking and cheating. My sisters became an important part of his life and so he started to commit some time to the family. My father had been a professional soccer player, and he expected my brother and me to follow his footsteps, although we did not agree with this idea. We both played soccer, but did not take it seriously; we saw other things as priorities. Growing up, church was a must, and our family followed the rules and traditions very rigorously: First Communion, Confession, the rules of Holy Week, and eating fish on Good Friday.

Throughout my walk as a child and consequently stepping into teenage years, I always had the vision to get ahead by my own means in all area of life: personal, financial, academic, and professional. I did not want anyone's help, I just wanted to work, make money and have a place of power - I am not really sure for what - but that is what I wanted. I started working at the age of six, selling lemons in the street; I probably inherited the deal-making skill from my father. I then worked for my father, and since then I have had a love for work, overall growth, and financial independence.

Coming into my teenage years was a unique experience. I had the vision of wanting to be a young, rich entrepreneur at a very early age; I did not have the maturity to take this role. I just wanted to have the ability to get a lot of money, help the poor, and be independent. I wanted to be seen as a noble figure of power. Throughout the years, I realize that was my empty vision. In my teenage years, I had many conflicting feelings and anxiety about the past, the present and the future. Although I despised my father's drinking, I started drinking at the age of 15. While I knew how much my mother suffered, I despised her for taking out her frustration on me, but at the same time I longed to get close to her.

In my teenage years, I remember getting a Bible once to read it. I started by reading in the Book of Revelation, which is a very scary book. After glancing through it, I closed it and did not come back to the Bible for many years. Deep inside of me, I always wanted to seek God; I just did not know how to do it. I was taught that contact with God was made through the priest, you followed their lead and that was it. I knew that there had to be something more than that; I just did not know what it was. I had been in search of God from a very young age, and I guess that by bits and pieces, I was being prepared to get to know God.

Towards the end of high school, I became very anxious about my future. I wanted to join the Air Force and this was my focus for most of the last school year. In the midst of working hard to accomplish my goal, however, I began a very intense relationship that eventually became intimate. It turned into an all-consuming obsession and because of it, I lost my focus of getting into the Air Force. I even came to the point of not caring about anything else but just being with my girlfriend. During this, my father and I began communicating, started repairing our relationship and learned to trust each other again.

I completed everything I was supposed to for the Air Force Academy, but in the end I did not want to go, and so did not. I had my girlfriend, and at the time that was all that mattered to me. After high school ended, my journey was clouded by the relationship; I lost track, and did not care. I was "in love". After about a year, my girlfriend got pregnant. I did not know what to do, but I was blessed to have my parents' support. This gave me confidence that everything would be fine.

A New Trek: from Colombia to the United States

After considering all the options, I decided to step away from the relationship. After all, I needed to provide for my daughter and I could not accomplish that without an education. I worked several jobs to try to generate an income to support my little girl, but it was not an easy task. I landed a job that paid a little over minimum wage and demanded many hours, so I could not go to school. My goal at that point was to get an education, but I saw that as a pipe dream. After exploring some possibilities, I decided to travel to the United States to study and work. The constants in my walk in life became the hunger for learning and the desire to support my daughter.

I arrived in the United States on August 18, 1998. It was a warm day. I was bewildered by the chaos of the airport, customs, the number of people rushing by, the language, and not being able to understand what was being said to me. It was very frustrating; I felt like I had traveled to another planet. I was by myself and was committed to staying until I had succeeded in getting a stable income and an education. There was no turning back for me, even though my family and I all suffered. It was painful that I had to be away from my daughter to be able to support her. It was an adjustment for everyone, but I knew that even though it was tough, that was the best choice and one that had already been made. I was determined to go to school, learn the language and start working. It was a very scary situation; I was 19 years old, and I had come to the U.S. by myself. I faced loneliness, becoming the target of racial jokes, and the adaptation of a new culture, new language and new traditions. It was like being born again.

I arrived in a small town called Gadsden, Alabama. This town will always carry a very special place in my heart. I went to school there and although there were some bad experiences, I also met people who were supportive and a blessing in my life, and in an interesting twist, wanted to share God with me.

God, Life in the World and a Recollection of the Past

Finding out there were people in a foreign land who cared about me was a surprise. I thought they just wanted something from me, but they genuinely showed their love. They helped with my homework and they shared prayers. I particularly remember Pastor Alan visiting with me to see how I was doing and to see how he could help. The people from the churches always demonstrated love by their actions instead of preaching. I later realized that God had started to work in my heart, to show what my future would be.

During my stay in Alabama, I took part in what I had despised in my younger years: alcohol consumption. There were always gatherings and the gatherings always had alcohol. At moments of desperation and distress, I joined the group of the alcoholics and eventually became one. Eventually, I lost focus of what I was supposed to be doing and had to move in with a relative to concentrate on school and getting a job. I later moved to New Jersey and then to Massachusetts. My life was in disarray, and I had many mixed feelings. I became familiar with the language and was able to somehow survive on my own, but still deep within me, I was in search of truth in life. I had lost track of things several times and I became angry with myself; I wanted to get ahead, not be a failure.

Steps to the Future: a Journey Towards Maturity

Once I settled in Massachusetts, I had the opportunity to attend a community college. After I tried and failed four times to pass English 101, the professor told me I was not college material. I believed that for several years. I continued working, yet with no college degree.

238

While working at a Fortune 500 financial institution, I learned about their tuition reimbursement program, and thought I should consider going back to school. I took the chance, and tried English 101 once more. This time though, I was more grounded and my reading and writing skills had improved. This class was harder than the previous four, but I was able to get an A+ for the class. This was a tremendous boost for my confidence, and the push I needed to continue my education journey.

I earned an undergraduate degree from Becker College, and five years later an MBA with dual specialization in finance and innovation entrepreneurship from Northeastern University. This was not unusual; I know of many people who have undergone similar or more challenging journeys, yet continue to push forward in the effort to attain their goals.

My wife, Mayra (the center of my life) and I have very similar journeys: we both came to the United States by ourselves, persevered in achieving a higher education, and set our hearts, souls, and minds to be good at what we do. My daughter came to live with us for about a year, and learned English while she was here. She decided to move back to Colombia and attend school there, pursuing a degree in accounting. She is strong, a natural leader, and is now part of the student representatives team at her University.

My wife and I have had the opportunity to face challenges. We have both grown and learned to manage these trials in thoughtful ways, and have thankfully been able to set a strong foundation for our future, our key to success has been to walk together, and overcome, we have done this many times, and this has made our relationship stronger and it has paved the way to us to continue growing our relationship.

We have both aimed to contribute in the journey of others in any way we can. She is a kindergarten teacher, and I have been blessed to work at Fortune 500 companies, entrusted with delivering value both individually and as a leader of a team. I have served on various boards, and volunteered to mentor, serve, and share my talents for the wellbeing of society.

This is just a snippet of my story. We are all unique, and face different challenges in our journey. The most important lesson I have learned is to not give up, to persevere despite the challenges. Always look up and ahead towards the goals we have set, so that we can all live a Trek of Purpose.

* * * * *

A Kick in the Gut

Alan Lindeman

First, I have to say that I am living a very blessed life. That's not to say that I do not have my fair share of trials and tribulations, but, in spite of the challenges, I am living a blessed life. You might ask why, and my answer is simply... I am married to the woman of my dreams, I have an amazing family, and I get to do what I love to do for a living. Even better, I am doing what the Good Lord has asked me to do – make a positive difference in the lives of people.

But looking back over my life, there were many years where I did not feel this way. In fact, there was a point several years ago when my life felt like the Rolling Stones song - *Satisfaction*. Remember the lyrics...

> *"...I can't get no satisfaction, I can't get no satisfaction*
> *'Cause I try and I try and I try and I try*
> *I can't get no, I can't get no..."*

I just felt an emptiness in my life - a void that was hard to describe. I definitely felt something was missing and I couldn't put my finger on it.

Before I go any further, I should probably share that my life wasn't filled with a huge amount of hardship and challenges. At least, no more than most people I know. I grew up in a nice suburban home with loving parents and three older brothers. I went to very good private schools. I had a number of very good friends. My first major hardship was the passing of my father when I was in college. In spite of that, I persevered with school and graduated on time. I married the love of my life a month after graduation and set off to tackle the world. For many years that is exactly what we did. I spent the next seventeen years working for four different companies, and with each new company came an opportunity to advance myself professionally. The fourth company afforded me my first management opportunity and I was so excited to get it.

You might be asking what the heck did I have to complain about? All I can say is that I still felt that something was missing. I could not put my finger on it, but there was a void - an empty feeling that I couldn't get over.

Things started to change in the spring of 1999 when I attended a Catholic Men's Conference in Cincinnati, Ohio. I attended the one-day event with a number of other dads from the church that I belonged to. One of the featured speakers was a young man named Matthew Kelly, who was an Australian born speaker and writer. As I was listening to him speak that day, it felt like something inside of me woke up. I had a new awareness about myself that started the process of changing my life and helped me to fill the emptiness I had been feeling.

In his speech, Matthew shared that every day we have a responsibility to ourselves and the world, to work on becoming better than we were the day before. He simply said that we need to "become a better version of ourselves" every day. I still can hear him say those words in his Australian accent. These words immediately touched my soul and woke something up inside me. It was one of those rare epiphanies we might be blessed with during our lives if we are lucky and awake. It caused me to realize how little I had invested in my own spiritual and mental development since I graduated from college.

For the next few days I kept going back to those words that Matthew had said about striving to become a better version of myself every day. The concept moved me enough to make a pretty big decision. I decided that I would wake up 30 minutes earlier each day to start reading his book "The Rhythm of Life" that I had purchased at the event. I would spend 20 minutes reading and then 10 minutes sitting quietly and thinking about what I read.

As I read with each passing day, I felt within me a ground-swell of confidence and motivation to do more. So much so that it even scared me some. I really didn't understand what was going on inside me, but I knew I needed to continue. The voice inside me kept telling me to keep reading.

From there, I decided to invest in a few more books. Beside Matthew Kelly's book, I bought *The 7 Habits of Highly Effective People, SPIN Selling, The E Myth*, and a few more. I was becoming a sponge for information and knowledge, and within a couple of weeks I was no longer reading for just 30 minutes in the morning. I would read or listen to books on business, sales, spirituality, and personal motivation for at least 60 minutes every day.

After a few weeks of reading on my own, I became inspired to share what I was studying with family and coworkers. I was encouraged by how receptive my team at work was. At first, I would just make a comment about a concept I had read about, which would lead to a casual conversation about it. Then, I started talking about what I was reading in a manager's meeting, or a sales meeting. Eventually, we decided to read and discuss a few books as a group. The interesting result was that we became a tighter group at work and there was a noticeable increase in activity and success with our business unit. Good things were happening.

Over time, I started to realize that I had developed a passion for learning. Even more surprising to me was that I really enjoyed sharing the information with others. As I would find a new "golden nugget" from my studies I would get so excited that I couldn't wait to share it with people on my team. It was fun, and together we all grew in so many ways.

In the 10 years following Matthew Kelly's speech in 1999, I sensed many times that there was a greater purpose behind the time I was spending on personal development. At the time I couldn't articulate it, but, as I look back, I know that God had a hand in what was going on in my life. As I was wrapping up one book, I would start looking for what was next. Sometimes I would be reading two to three different books at the same time. I would usually read a spiritual book in the morning and business books during lunch and in the evening.

Then, in early 2009 some big changes happened in my professional life. In January, I was told that the company was launching a new division and they wanted me to join it in a business development capacity. This move would allow the owner's son the opportunity to move into his first management opportunity – the role I had filled for the previous seventeen years.

Over the course of 2009 and 2010, as I was working to develop business opportunities for the new division, I realized how much I missed working with the team I led for so many years. I missed the opportunities to share what I had been reading and learning about. I missed using my growth to help my team grow. I started to understand that my passion for learning had evolved into a passion for teaching, coaching, and mentoring. Unfortunately, my new position didn't provide as many opportunities to do what I now loved to do – teach.

Another big change in my life took place in 2010 - I met Tim Burgess. Tim was leading a study group on Napoleon Hill's classic book *Think and Grow Rich*. I had started to read the book several times during the previous ten years but never could finish it. I joined the study group and was amazed at the power of the material in the book, as well as Tim's knowledge and understanding of the material. I later found out that he had been studying *Think and Grow Rich* every day for fifteen years. After the second session, I asked Tim where he lived and found out we lived fairly close to one another. A week later we met for breakfast and instantly became friends. Tim introduced me to new books and programs from people like Napoleon Hill, Bob Proctor, *The Secret*, and so much more.

By the end of 2010, I approached the leadership of my company with an idea. I wanted to spend a small percentage of my time (10 to 20%) coaching and mentoring people, while I spent the lion's share of my time on business development. I explained how much I enjoyed teaching, and how I could help the company groom people for playing larger roles within the business. We went back and forth with my idea for several months. The week after Thanksgiving of 2011 I had a meeting with the president of the company, who informed me that they were eliminating my position.

Wow! What a kick in the gut. I had spent over twenty years committing myself to the company and they were showing me to the door. What kind of thanks is that? I gave most of my adult life to this company and they are telling me to go away!?

At first, I was pretty devastated and deeply hurt. But, over the course of a few weeks I started to sense that what they did to me was a blessing in disguise. I left my position in January and immediately started interviewing with a variety of companies. At the same time, I began to see that my new situation also created a whole new opportunity to do what I loved to do – teach – but on a whole new level. In May of 2012, I told the last of the companies I was considering, "No thank you" - I was going to start my own training and consulting business. My friend Tim Burgess and I had decided to work together doing sales and leadership training for companies in the Cincinnati area.

By the end of 2013, Tim and I decided to become full partners and created Maximizing Results. Our simple mission as a business is to help individuals, companies, and organizations become better versions of themselves so that they can produce better results – personally and professionally. It is curious how much those words I heard Matthew Kelly say back in 1999 have impacted my life.

I set out to build a business that allows me to make a positive difference in people's lives by teaching the concepts and principles I had learned over the many years. What I discovered through this was my calling in life. God's purpose for me is to teach and coach people and companies, to help them learn how to achieve the results they desire.

It's been five years since I left the corporate world. I look back and can say I do not miss it. I don't miss it because every day I get to do what I love to do. I get to help people become better versions of themselves, so that they can go achieve what they want in their lives. The truth is, I have found my passion, and it is amazing.

It's All Homework

Michelle Sager

Do you remember where you and your children spent Spring Break week in 2008? Was it at Disney? On a beach? Fishing at the lake? Visiting the big city museums and theaters?

I remember where I spent mine, and it wasn't any of those places. It was the art room and cafeteria at my daughter's elementary school, without my daughter. I spent the whole week with some of my favorite women setting up for the school's Art Show that was taking place the next week. Five days of stapling artwork to large sheets of paper to hang in the hallways. Four to five projects for each child, times three classrooms of students in each of the five grades came out to a lot of art! It was something the PTA (Parent/Teacher Association) had always gladly done for the art teacher; this year a scheduling snafu required us to prepare over break. It was to be one of the last times I spent at the school.

I was President of the elementary PTA, having held other positions over the past six years. I was also on the PTA Executive Board at the middle school. My husband served on an exploratory committee for school district funding and restructuring. I was a Math and Reading tutor for the 2nd grade classrooms. I volunteered in the cafeteria. When the office was busy, I answered the phone. We had advocated for the school funding amendment to the Ohio Constitution. We joined. We volunteered. We cared. We helped. We advocated.

We didn't do it for gold stars, awards, gift cards, or applause. Everything we did was to try to make the schools the best they could be for our children. Our children, and all the other children in the district. But, honestly, our own children were our first priority. Is that selfish? I don't think so. As parents, we had an instinct to protect our own children, and help them thrive. Every parent does. Or should.

I was at the elementary school a lot. Every. Single. Day. Sometimes I went to school with my daughter, and she stayed after school until I finished whatever I was working on. I will never ask another person to do something I am not willing to do myself...so I pitched in to help wherever I was needed.

As President of the PTA, I had access to, and the ear of, the school Principals, the District Superintendent, some of the School Board Members, and many, many wonderful teachers in both schools. The more I learned about the public-school system, the more I *learned*. The further I got into the what, why, and how of government schools, the more I disliked the system. Teachers having no autonomy in their own classrooms. Not able to teach the way their kids learn. Just because the class of 22, or 30, or 35 kids are in the same grade doesn't make them the same. They aren't all ready for the same information at the same time, and do not all learn at the same pace, or in the same way. The more I saw, the more frustrated I became.

Our school district tested children for giftedness as early as Kindergarten, but did nothing to support the children until 4th grade. Our son had been part of the gifted program in the 4th and 5th grade, and we loved his teacher. The program was tailored to the children and allowed our son to explore, grow and thrive. At the middle school, however, gifted classes just meant more work, faster. Busy work. The same curriculum the other children were learning, just faster. That's an accelerated class, not gifted. He hated it. Our daughter wasn't being served either; just an occasional pull-out from 2nd grade to a math class doing 4th grade work. She was bored with 2nd grade and getting into trouble for talking. And the homework. So much homework for both of them, and it seemed like material they should have been learning at school.

Our children are immersion learners. They would perform the requested tasks and did their assignments quickly. They usually read ahead in the textbooks, while waiting for the next lesson. If they weren't interested in the topic, they would grow weary of the repetition and act out. Then, of course, they didn't want to do the homework – it was something they already knew and didn't want to repeat. If something intrigued them, they would immerse themselves in learning everything they could about it, until dragged along to the next topic by the scheduled curriculum. They were both frustrated that they couldn't spend less time waiting for the class to move on, and more time learning about things that interested them.

As I said, everything we did, we did for our children. But quite often what we did wasn't *with our children*. And it wasn't what they needed. They didn't need a better Spring Carnival, or more fun at Donuts with Dad. They needed a better learning environment, and they needed me.

Right after Christmas Break, I had been chatting with a friend and fellow PTA Mom whose twin boys were in my daughter's 2nd grade class. Her boys were "too spirited for the classroom" – and I think, bored with 2nd grade, just like my daughter. She was telling me about a program she was considering signing up for: she could teach her kids at home and this company would send her everything she needed to do it. When they finished 3rd grade, they could move on to 4th without waiting for the next school year, or even each other. Intrigued, I got started researching homeschool methods: at the library, online, and the bookstore. I talked to a couple of people that I knew homeschooled. I also looked into some charter and private schools in our area, just to make sure I had the information I needed. At first, I was doing all of the research myself and hadn't yet involved my husband. Again, the more I learned, the more *I learned.*

While stapling artwork for the Art Show, I was again talking with my friend. We were considering a move to Tennessee at the end of the school year, and I didn't have enough information yet on the school system in the area. I had already done all the research for our current location. She had made the decision to teach all four of her kids at home the next year, not just the twins. We talked about how she planned to do it, including books, online work, field trips, clubs, sports, etc. for her kids. She had gotten her kids' input on a lot of things that they were going to do. The longer she talked, the more this little voice in my head told me that was the answer: *Talk to Bob. Talk to the kids. Show them your research. Answer their questions. Ask your own. Then you can decide.*

I did. We did.

We spent the summer in a small apartment preparing for the move to Tennessee, and kept up the same type of schedule we had in previous summers. Visits to the zoo, museums, parks, movies, an amusement park. We played games, swam, took mini trips, and visited friends. Every day we also worked in our summer learning workbooks, as we had every other year. They are designed to keep kids from the "summer slide": that condition of mushy brain that happens at the beginning of every school year. We kept up the homeschool journals we had started: we wrote down concerns, goals, questions, things we were excited about, worried about, hated, loved, looked forward to, would miss.

In September, we set off on a new adventure together. We moved to a small house in a nice neighborhood near Maryville, Tennessee. We arrived in the middle of the night:

it took a long time to drive a moving truck over the mountains from Cincinnati, Ohio. The next day, when the kids went outside, they immediately had a new passel of friends. We were going to love it there.

When school began for us, we read together and separately. They read fiction and non-fiction: any topic they wanted, and some that I requested. We took weekly visits to the library. Wrote poetry, watched plays. They had a class called "Vocabulary with Dad." Spelling and vocabulary words became crossword puzzles and word finds. They wrote stories and essays. PowerPoints, presentations, and videos were created to present their research. We went on field trips, created a history timeline, did math. The dining room was filled with flashcards, games, paper, science fair boards, markers, pens, crayons, glue, and books, book, books.

There were no also more fights over hours and hours of homework to keep the kids inside every evening instead of playing in the beautiful, mild weather.

Was it all fabulous? No! For the first year, the kids would ask me every day when "school" was over so they could do something else. We had a lot of togetherness that we weren't used to. Some of what we did looked like "school" and some of it didn't. We tried things that failed. I purchased books we never used. The kids hated some of our time together, I was frustrated and we seemed to be in a rut.

One day I was looking through my journal and came across something that reminded me why we decided to homeschool in the first place: *I want my children to develop a lifelong love of learning, and learn how to think, not what to think.*

Change of plans. We ditched school and decided to learn.

We incorporated life into learning instead of dividing life from "school." This meant all learning, including family trips, chores, videos, music lessons, family game night, and the dinnertime discussion about the museum we visited last week all counted as school. It made it easier to show the children how things fit together. Since life doesn't happen in a vacuum, it isn't divided neatly into subjects. It only makes sense to learn as a whole. We engaged the children in the process of planning, developing, and evaluating their own experiences. They shared with us what they learned, by telling us what they learned. Sounds kind of sensible, when you stop and think about it.

A couple of years later, we moved back to Ohio. We changed our home base, but not our homeschool philosophy.

We have taken "school" trips all over - to Indianapolis to visit all of the war museums, to the Budweiser plant and Grant's Farm in St. Louis. The kids have been to Colonial Williamsburg, Jamestown and Yorktown, Las Vegas Motor Speedway and Hoover Dam, Hilton Head Island, and Savannah. All of these family vacations have been learning experiences. We've done science in the kitchen and outside. Math at the grocery and in a book. Piano, American Sign Language, and Art. A study of the Three Kingdoms Period in China, and Shakespeare. We play Risk, Scrabble, Checkers and Boggle. Historical movies, documentaries, Spanish, German and Chinese. Architecture. Chemistry, Biology and Anatomy. We learn "regular" class topics, just not in a regular way.

Our son graduated in 2014 and our daughter is beginning her last year of high school this year (2017). We have been homeschoolers for nine years now, and I am both happy and sad this year is our last.

Our son still immerses himself in whatever topic interests him and learns everything he can until he runs it out. With his knowledge base, work ethic, moral center and drive to know, he can do anything he wants with his life.

Our daughter still learns a new word-a-day, and shares them with her Dad. She has a lot of passions and can spend hours learning about the movie industry, science, languages, literature. Her biggest dilemma is finding the time for everything.

It has been quite a journey we have taken together; we have learned right along with the kids, and they have developed a love of learning. I think we have been successful – we have taught them how to think, not what to think. The time we have spent together is irreplaceable, our focus and goals have changed, and it's all homework.

* * * * *

My Hurricane

Yvette Adams

In September of 1989, I was in my Junior year of college at the University of South Carolina. It was announced that the campus was being evacuated because a hurricane was coming. Being from New York City and only 20 at the time, I had no genuine appreciation for the devastation of a hurricane. Fortunately for me, that same year my parents had moved to South Carolina after my dad retired. This allowed me to go home and be with my family during the storm. It was still frightening to me; the rain was coming down in sheets and the blowing wind was bending the trees almost to breaking.

That night was difficult, as I was overcome with fear and anxiety. The lights flickered on and off, and eventually never came back on. Hugo arrived in the early morning hours. The wind was howling, and the sheets of rain were slamming against the house, creating a slapping sound against the windows and sliding glass doors. I was intermittently startled by loud cracking sounds, that I found later to be trees breaking and crashing into power lines, homes and the ground. The darkness from the dark grey and blue-black sky was suffocating as there was no street lights to even cast a shadow.

That day, while the sky showed us a peek of beautiful sunshine, my father and I ventured out to my first-and-only experience of going to an ice house to buy blocks of ice. On the way, we saw trees uprooted, power lines down and homes destroyed. I began to cry as I saw the destruction, wondering whether the people were alright. There were trees lying in the middle of houses and cars upside down. This was the first time in my young life I felt true pain for others in my community.

Once we arrived at the ice house, I was fascinated watching the workers use a pick and some sort of hammer to break the large blocks of ice into manageable square and rectangle chunks. When we returned home, my father put them into coolers with our food, and my mother began grilling meats on the patio. Thank God for old school ways when devastation comes. Mother cooked outside on that beautiful day. We ate well, and then readied ourselves as the sky began to darken, once again. We faithfully rode out the rest of storm with total respect and humility for what Hugo was bringing on its tail.

Several years later, while pregnant with my first child, I was on a tour at the Congaree National Forest in South Carolina. The tour guide showed us how the boardwalk was built by the trees that had fallen, and looking over the boardwalk we saw large roots of old majestic trees laid down by Hurricane Hugo. What stuck in my mind the most that day was the beauty of the new vegetation growing. The tour guide explained that the trees had previously created a canopy that shielded the sun from shining on the soil, and prevented new growth. So, although violently destructive, the hurricane had created an environment for new life to grow. Previously hidden seeds had been lying dormant, just waiting for the sun to shine on them.

Little did I know then that I would experience, years later, my own hurricane. My brother was diagnosed with cancer and died within a year; my father was diagnosed with cancer a year later, and experienced a slow decline of two years which resulted in his death as well. My marriage ended during the period of Poppy's illness, and the same year of his death I was kidnapped and assaulted. This was more than a just series of unfortunate events. To complicate matters I was diagnosed with a chronic disease as well. With four children to raise and feeling totally beaten by life, all I could feel was devastation.

It was during this time that I was diagnosed both with Post Traumatic Stress Disorder and mild agoraphobia. This gave me some of the answers that I needed. Now I knew that the flashbacks, depression and anxiety I was experiencing were a natural reaction to abnormal events. Fortunately, I met a wonderful group of people, who helped me retain the normalcy in my life. With the help of Sistercare, an organization for abused women and children, I began to heal.

I received counseling and the best play therapists for my children, a legal advocate, and a social worker to help me gently with the guidance of doctors and a psychologist specializing in PTSD. These women became my safety net and provided the tools, encouragement and hope for me to rebuild. The sun began to shine on the soil of my soul. My children were my inspiration to continue, however difficult; to fertilize that soil, to not give up hope and allow something bigger than simply surviving to develop - something much greater than healing to begin.

A period of self-discovery was beginning. My mother's lap was always available for tears as she wiped my forehead, prayed and gave me words of wisdom, understanding and strength. Grandmother was a rock of love, and faith and an unwavering belief in the beauty and greatness in me and children. I had two aunts - total opposites of each other - one sharing faith, God and encouragement; while the other was the soldier and bodyguard at the hospitals, police stations and court rooms. These great women never tired of nurturing and watering my thirsty soul. God placed me in an environment of safety, with wonderful, psychologists, psychiatrists and counselors that gave me tools to grow. My children were the sun and rain that watered it. These relationships were so powerful in my beginning to thrive in life.

I have learned to fear no man, woman or opportunity. Sometimes we must start over to grow. Today I work for myself, and have successfully homeschooled my children, remarried and have a one-year-old son. I have learned that life is for the living. Hurricanes can provide opportunity for new life to begin. I have found my creative, confident and persistent self. I also learned that no one is an island. Although I still have flashbacks sometimes, they are placed where they belong; as memories, just like Hurricane Hugo. There is no more destruction, just new life, peace and prosperity.

Very Scary Movie Night

Bob Sager

When I was young I was athletic. From the time I was 10 years old, I spent hour after hour on the basketball court. It didn't matter if the temperature was 89° or 29°. A group of friends and I even had what we called the 'polar bear club'. It was a group of the heartiest and most committed basketball enthusiasts. We even cleaned snow off the court to play. Like most teenage boys, I had boundless amounts of energy.

Then, *life* happened. After high school, there were no more organized sports for me to participate in. Some of the members of the polar bear club joined the military, some went on to play college basketball, and some just sort of got lost in the wind. Playing basketball one on *none* isn't very enjoyable. And, pick-up games without my buddies around definitely lacked the luster that our old games had. When the fun has gone out of the game, it's just exercise. And, who wants to do that? I know I really didn't. I never understood how people can just run. For fun. Still don't.

On top of that, a funny thing happened to my metabolism once I graduated from puberty. It slowed down, big time! But, I still had the same eating habits that had been ingrained over the course of several years. Also, as an adult I decided what to buy at the grocery store. That's where my biggest problem occurred.

It's important to say here, that while I was growing up, my family was borderline poor. Oh, we never went hungry, at least not that I remember. But, one thing required of everyone in our house was getting out and sweating, breaking our backs and getting chewed on by all sorts of malicious critters. This thrill ride was called 'working in the garden.' No one likes to be forced to do things, but working in the garden wasn't optional. I realize looking back, that our very large garden was the only reason we had half of the food we ate. I still remember telling my mother that once I grew up, I would NEVER have a garden. I was going to make enough money to buy everything I wanted at the grocery store.

Side Note: I have never planted a garden, and still to this day, working in dirt, pulling weeds and getting chewed on by critters while doing it is my own personal version of hell. I only do such things because I love my wife and she likes to plant flowers. But, I digress.

I'm firmly convinced that one of the reasons I bought the kinds of foods I did as an adult is because I had none of them growing up. Prepared foods and microwavable meals weren't an option (we had no microwave). Soda was an extremely rare thing in our house, as were items such as cookies and candy. I started doing things to make money when I was 10 years old, and used to spend some of my money on candy and root beer. When I started making better money and was in control of what came home, these junk food items became a staple. By the way, don't get me wrong: I'm not down on fatty, sugary and relatively unhealthy items. It's just a bad idea to make those a part of your every-day diet.

It doesn't take a rocket scientist to figure out what the results were of several years of dramatically less exercise, a slowing metabolism and poor eating habits. I had gone from being athletic, to being really overweight and out of shape. But, I didn't really notice that much.

If you've been out of high school or college for more than a few years, you've probably had this experience. You get reacquainted with a friend on social media and you barely recognize them from their picture. They just don't look like they did those many years ago. Because the difference in their appearance is so stark, it's almost shocking how much different they look. But, it's a funny thing; when you're around someone all the time, you tend not to notice those gradual changes. And, like everyone, I was with myself 24/7/365. The pounds kept adding up, and I mostly just ignored them.

Then came the weekend that was like a cold slap in the face!

We have a tradition in our household. The Saturday night immediately before Halloween we celebrate with what we call 'Sager Family Scary Movie Night.' This tradition involves watching age-appropriate 'ghost-y' movies. For the younger children, this could be *Elmo Says Boo* or *Wishbone's* version of *Sleepy Hollow,* and for the older children and adults it's something a bit more intense.

What would a movie night be without all sorts of food? And, boy did we have food! We would make two or three casserole-dish sized hot foods, several kinds of cheeses and various crackers, chips, dips, cookies and candy. Naturally, there were plenty of calorie-filled beverages as well. It was a table-full and a counter-full. Sort of like a Thanksgiving of junk food.

When the kids were still of trick-or-treating age, part of the tradition was to let them dress up in their Halloween costumes to watch the movies. This night was no different. What was different was for the first time we had a video camera to capture the magic in moving pictures. We recorded the kids having fun, hanging out in their costumes and eating. Fortunately for me, the children weren't the only ones being recorded.

The next day we all wanted to watch the previous night's fun that we had captured on video. So, we turned on the television and began to watch. The kids looked like they were having fun and it was amusing reliving the events of the night before. Until...there was a shot of me eating something. A full body shot. A *really* full body shot! It was a shocking moment I'll never forget. Like when you see someone you haven't seen in years and you barely recognize them. I was hit right in the eyes with the truth. Do you know the old saying; 'The truth shall set you free?' Well, it will. The part they don't tell you is first it upsets you. For me, *upset* is not a strong enough word. I was in shock!

I looked at myself on video and said, "Holy Crap! I'm FAT!"

It was like an alarm went off in my head. This was almost 20 years ago and I still remember it like it happened last week.

I immediately thought, 'If I don't lose some weight – a lot of weight – I'm not even going to be around to see my grandchildren.' For me at least, there was something about facing the prospect of an early death that snapped me into a different mindset.

I put a game plan in place. Notice I did not say 'a diet.' It was my personal experience that diets don't work. You see, I wasn't completely unaware that I had gained weight over the years, I just didn't know how much. I had tried 'diets' of various kinds in the past. I'd lose a few pounds and feel good. Then, I'd gradually resume the same old eating habits and gain all the weight back – and then some. No, I did not need a diet. I needed a change in the way I ate and approached food. The game plan was simple. I called it the 'half' plan. I took the amount of food I was used to eating and cut it in half. If we had cheeseburgers for dinner, I had one instead of two. Second helpings were out. If we got take-out pizza, I'd have two slices rather than four. It was simple. I had obviously been eating twice as much food as I needed for years.

The only part that took any will power was the first week or two when my body was adjusting to the drop in food intake. I figured out that food can be like a drug. The more you have, the more your body expects. And it builds up an expectation of how much should be ingested. Just like a drug addict builds up a tolerance for whatever substance is being abused, and more and more is needed to elicit the same response, you get used to eating a certain amount. When that amount is not forthcoming, the body objects! I knew that once I adjusted my body's expectations, I wouldn't feel those pangs of hunger. And, I was right. After the first couple of weeks of my 'half' plan, I was no longer hungry.

Something else I did differently than my past 'diets' - I did not change what I ate. I only changed the amounts. For example, I still had desserts. But, instead of having desserts five or six days a week, I had dessert twice; Sunday and Wednesday. For me – and I believe for a lot of other people – one of the reasons that diets never work is that the entire time you're 'on a diet' you feel like you are depriving yourself. If you're used to a particular type of food and you quit it cold-turkey, it's unlikely you'll stick with eating the new foods. Even if you do stick with it long enough, through sheer will-power (a rarity), once your weight goal is reached, you'll return to eating the way you did before you deprived yourself into losing weight. However, it's been my experience that it is much easier to adjust to eating an amount of food that allows you to get to and maintain a desired weight.

After the Very Scary Movie Night slapped me into making a change, I lost 65 pounds over the next 18 months. And, for the most part, I've maintained that for almost 20 years and counting. If I ever feel my pants getting a little tight, I begin to monitor more closely the amounts I'm eating.

If you've had one of those, 'Holy crap, I'm FAT' moments like I did, take heart. You can transform your body the way I did. A little at a time, without depriving yourself. All you have to do is decide that you want to live! You'll probably even live to see your grandchildren – like I have. And, once you look better and have more energy, your quality of life will go dramatically up! If I can do it, so can you!

Meet the Authors

Matthew Orlando has been in sales and marketing for nearly two decades, the last ten of which has been in various leadership roles for companies in the insurance and healthcare industries. Since 2014, Matthew has been the Chief Executive Officer of IAM Insurance Agent, a leading marketing company in the insurance and financial industries. His company help firms recruit and sell products to insurance advisors through cutting-edge marketing platforms.

Matthew's road to obtaining success was rocky to say the least. His parents divorced at an early age and many of the lessons learned as a child carried through to his marriage where he repeated his parents' mistakes. His story is about a man who made a conscious decision to end the vicious cycle before it destroyed his relationship with his daughter.

www.IAmInsuranceAgent.com

* * * * *

Amazon #1 best-selling authors of *The Prosperity Factor*, and authors of *Couples Money*, **Chris and Marlow Felton** have inspired thousands of couples and financial professionals across the country. Chris and Marlow have 30 plus years combined experience in the financial services industry working with couples of all walks of life. They share their personal story of financial transformation and how they were able to go from struggling and fighting to financial harmony. Chris and Marlow have helped thousands of couples have easier and more productive conversations about money and teach powerful concepts to help couples make better financial decisions.

Chris and Marlow mentor and train over 200 financial professionals in their business across the country and are highly respected public speakers. They are recognized as leaders in the financial services industry and have presented for thousands of financial professionals all over the country. They are also highly sought-after speakers because of their unique perspective on wealth and helping people make a financial shift.

Chris and Marlow take an introspective approach to wealth and believe wealth is built from the inside out, based on 10 plus years of intense personal development and personal transformation. They have been students of numerous programs that have taught them not only how to transform their own life, but how to inspire others to make positive changes in their life.

www.CouplesMoney.com

* * * * *

Colby Richards is the Managing Partner of Brown Box Branding's Seattle office. He pours his expertise into helping others elevate their brands through engaging Web Design and Digital Marketing. His past experiences in media, industrial settings, and the insurance industry have given unique insight to the vast array of issues faced by those in business and in life. In his years with Brown Box Branding, he has worked to help grow his organization from one up to four locations nationwide.

Many life lessons have strengthened Colby's resilience. His story centers around what could have helped him avoid some of the more painful lessons as well as what helps him now navigate more effectively when things don't go as planned.

Colby resides near Seattle, Washington, with his wife and 4 children.

www.BrownBoxBranding.com/Seattle

* * * * *

Isabella Manetti lives on the Gold Coast, Australia. Her heritage is Italian and German. Earlier in her career she worked for corporate and government departments; initially as a personal assistant then assisting in development and promotion of environmental projects for the Queensland Government. She moved to Rome in 2011 to study Italian full-time and to learn more about her Italian culture. She returned to the Gold Coast in 2013 to start an online business that she was passionate about - personal development and spirituality.

Her company's name is Bella Vita 4 Life. She became an accredited Transformative Life Coach trained through "Inspired Spiritual Coaching Academy" where she learned coaching skills using the Law of Attraction principles. She has created many mind-body guided affirmation recordings and offers personalised visualisation and affirmation recordings all embedded with Theta Brainwave Entrainment Binaural Beats to fast track and enhance your results. She also has a presence on Facebook, YouTube, Instagram and Twitter and publishes a magazine app "BellaVita4Life".

You can find out more about Isabella Manetti at her website

www.createanewmindset.com.

* * * * *

Malavika Vivek is the executive director of Girls Make Apps, a national non-profit organization that seeks to bridge the gender gap in STEM by creating free programs and workshops across the country for middle-school-college women. As a senior at the Middlesex County Academy in New Jersey, she is extremely passionate about science, technology and social entrepreneurship. For her efforts to close the gender gap in technology, she has been recognized as a national runner-up by the National Center for Women and Information Technology as well as a 2017 Stanford #include fellow.

In Living a Wealthy Life, she shares about finding your passion and the lessons she's learned on her journey toward satisfaction. Her story has also been featured by several organizations like ReigningIt, Future Sharks, InTheirShoes and Overdressed and Overeducated. Her inspiring journey goes to show you that it is always the right time to make a change in your life and will help you start on the road towards personal satisfaction and happiness.

More about Girls Make Apps: www.facebook.com/GirlsMakeApps

* * * * *

268

Spike Humer is a Soul Advocate, entrepreneur, seeker, author, speaker, business leader, husband, father, son, brother and poet.

Spike is widely-recognized as a thought-leader and world-renowned expert in leading and inspiring companies, organizations, and individuals to achieve more, have more, and be more. He's been called the "mentor's mentor" and is highly regarded as a master marketing strategist and performance acceleration expert. Spike serves as a trusted advisor and performance consultant to entrepreneurs and individuals from virtually every walk-of-life and in countless industries.

From Wall Street to Main Street, from boardrooms and beyond Spike Humer has been at the forefront of business and the personal growth industry for the past 25 years. His explosive growth strategies for entrepreneurs, small businesses, and multi-million-dollar organizations as well as his unique and driven formulas for personal growth have made Spike one of the most important persons to know in the speaking, and consulting arena. Spike's programs, group mentoring, and personal consultations have gained the respect of tens of thousands.

Spike's been a featured speaker at seminars, business acceleration workshops around the world. He's shared the stage and program platforms with such business luminaries and thought-leaders as Jack Welch, Prime Minister Tony Blair, Stephen Covey, Seth Godin, Dr. Kevin Hogan, Mark Victor Hansen, Joe Sugarman, John Assaraf, Brendon Burchard, Darren J. Stephens, Chet Holmes, and many others. Spike has been applauded for his proven profit-boosting methodologies and "real-world" results-enhancement strategies for creating instant and lasting change in life and business.

Regarded by many as a leader and example of what's possible through "designed alignment" Spike continues to guide groups, organizations, and individuals in maximizing their potential and performance.

Currently, his time, attention, and passion is in spreading his wisdom and experiences in the forthcoming book *The Book of the Soul: How to rediscover and reconnect with your authentic self.*

www.TheBookofTheSoul.com

* * * * *

Beth Perkel wrote her first fiction novel manuscript at age 15, was published in her first major national and international magazines by age 17, won her first writing award at age 18 and had her writing featured in a New York Times bestselling book by age 19. Since then, she has continued to write articles, stories, web content and first-person essays for a dozen online and print publications as well as a parenting-meets-positive-psychology blog about teaching children happiness in the modern era.

A Phi Beta Kappa graduate of the University of Pennsylvania, she is a teacher, speaker, mediator, freelance writer and mother of four young children in Chicago, IL. You can connect with Beth on LinkedIn.

She is currently working on publishing her first fiction novel and you can read an excerpt on her website https://pollackbeth.wixsite.com/treadingwater .

* * * * *

Craig Fernandes spent the first 30 years of his career as a Marketing/Sales Executive working for leaders in the medical device industry. His most recent 20-year stint allowed him to settle down in Knoxville, TN where he has raised his family and enjoyed the Smoky Mountains. It's also where he became an avid fan of college football in the Volunteer State.

Craig now runs a consulting business where he helps aspiring entrepreneurs and offers sound advice to business start-ups across a broad range of industries. In his story, Craig shares the behind-the-scenes story of how he partnered with his teenage son Brady, to build Patriot Threads, one of America's most philanthropic and patriotic lifestyle apparel brands.

Patriot Threads measures their success as a company by the impact they have on the lives of others, and specifically on the lives of our Veterans.

www.PatriotThreads.org

* * * * *

Mark Brodinsky grew up in the suburbs just outside Baltimore, Maryland. His dream was to be on television and despite a stutter which affected most of his life, he managed to live that dream. During his senior year at Towson State University where he majored in Mass Communications, Mark got an internship at a local station, WJZ. He was hired as a writer and producer and eventually earned a spot as an On-Air talent (feature reporter) in 1991. Mark went on to work at the TV station for 15 years, earning an Emmy Award in 1996.

Despite his love of writing and performing, Mark eventually left TV to become self-employed and take control of his hours and his time for his growing family. But he never forgot about his love of performing and writing. When his wife was diagnosed with breast cancer in April of 2012, Mark kept an online journal on Caringbridge, documenting the cancer journey from a spouse's perspective. The posts were followed by many who encouraged him to turn it into a book. The book, *It Takes 2. Surviving Cancer: A Spouse's Story* became an Amazon #1 Best Seller. Mark also started a worldwide blog called *It's Just About... Life & The Sunday Series*. *The Sunday Series* are weekly stories of courage, hope and inspiration - real people overcoming real challenges which inspired us all. After securing more than 150 stories on the blog, Mark published a compilation book of the best of the first 50 stories in his newest book, *The Sunday Series with Mark Brodinsky. Real Stories of Courage, Hope & Inspiration,Volume I.*

Mark has also launched a storytelling and speaking business, where he tells stories to help businesses attract new clients and nonprofits to attract donors and to increase donor engagement. A voracious learner of personal development and self-improvement. Mark also has a motivational speaking program called Lasting Change: Change Your Story. Change Your Life – how little things you can do consistently each day – which are easy to do and easy not to do – can lead to big improvements in your life.

www.Markbrodinsky.com

* * * * *

At the age of 23, **Nancy Ward** started in a direct sales business that would give her more than she imagined. As a Pampered Chef consultant, her passion inspired others to learn how to cook and even want to cook. While selling these top-notch cooking tools, she earned commission, and she grew her wealth. Many of the hosts, customers and consultants she has met over the years she considers friends, some even close friends.

With a Bachelor's in Business Administration, Nancy has used her marketing skills over the years in her business, for the PTO at her children's schools, organizing effective silent auctions at church and school, and running gymnastics meets for the booster club. During the school year, she mentors her daughter's Girl Scout troop, which she has been leading since they were kindergarten Daisies. In her free time, Nancy enjoys travelling and working on her scrapbooks.

As a single mom, Nancy understands the importance of time management, being watchful of money, but also make memories when you can and be grateful for what you have.

www.pamperedchef.biz/nancychef

* * * * *

Michael Davis, the Storytelling MD, works with executives to improve their public speaking and communication skills. His passion for working with others is born from an experience in first grade that for 25 years kept him from speaking in front of others. He has taken the proven processes and tools learned from the best communicators in the world and packaged them into his own processes.

He is the author of *THE Book on Storytelling*, the Kindle book series *Sell More With Stories*, and is a contributing author to the Amazon #1 Bestselling *World Class Speaking in Action*.

To keep abreast of new ideas from the speaking world, he works closely with World Champion and Hall of Fame speakers, a leading Hollywood scriptwriting consultant, TED X Cincinnati and an award-winning Las Vegas headliner. Because of his dedication to the craft, Michael is sought by speakers all over the world.

If you'd like to accelerate your storytelling skills, sign up for Michael's complementary storytelling tips. For one year, you'll receive a weekly five-minute audio tip. Each one builds upon previous lessons. To register, visit:

52StorytellingTips.com

* * * * *

Kwame Christian Esq., M.A. is a awyer who focuses on serving the needs of small businesses. He graduated from the top ranked dispute resolution program in the country and he was recognized by the American Bar Association for his success in regional and national negotiation competitions during law school. He also founded and operates a consulting firm that specializes in teaching entrepreneurs and professionals how to negotiate in the business world and resolve disputes.

Kwame also hosts the podcast *Negotiate Anything*, the top ranked negotiation podcast on iTunes, where he interviews successful entrepreneurs and shares powerful persuasion techniques. After only 10 months, the show has been downloaded over 28,000 times by listeners in 63 different countries and was recently featured on the homepage of iTunes.

www.KChristianLaw.com

www.AmericanNegotiationInstitute.com

* * * * *

Karynne Summars is a former international corporate finance professional turned author, screenwriter, freelance journalist and film producer.

She is a contributing writer for several international magazines. Her feature articles cover entertainment and culture as well as international travel and personal development.

With her image and personal development advice book *Your Image Determines Your Success*, she would like to give people of all ages the tools to redesign their life and become more creative.

She is an avid traveler and engaged in various international cultural and entertainment activities.

Born and raised in Berlin, Germany, Karynne currently resides mainly in New York with additional residences in Berlin, Germany and Marbella, Spain.

www.KarynneSummars.com

www.facebook.com/ImageDeterminesSuccess/

Follow on Twitter www.Twitter.com/Karynne_Summars .

Visit Karyanne's IMDb page:
http://www.imdb.com/name/nm6157144/

* * * * *

Leroy Reshard brings over 27 years of professional sales and mentoring experience from 3M where he consistently ranked in the top 5 – 10% of 3M sales representatives. His achievement, mentoring and leadership skills earned an appointment to the position of account executive; the highest position for sales reps. A position held by less than 5% of all 3M reps. It's reserved for the best of the best! In 2001, he took early retirement to spend more time with family and focus on entrepreneurial opportunities.

Since retirement, he's opened a State Farm Insurance Agency; serves as a Business Development Manager/Fundraiser for Butler County United Way and Business Development Officer with First Financial Bank in Ohio. In 2007, he started LAPS Sales Training as an independent consultant to help companies and individuals grow and develop sales by using the knowledge, processes and skills he learned at 3M. Leroy loves to share his passion for helping others achieve results beyond their expectations.

As a Franchise Business Consultant, Leroy loves to help executives, professionals and veterans find the right franchise business for their background, skills and personality. Military experience is a great asset and many Franchisors offer a pricing discount to Veterans!

Leroy is a native of Tallahassee, Florida where he was first educated in the Reshard Family School of hard knocks, high character and strong work ethic. He moved to Hempstead, NY to become an electrician, his childhood dream. As a Veteran of the US Army and a recipient of the Bronze Star, Leroy attended Nassau Community and Hofstra University full time at night while working full time during the day. His college expenses were paid by the GI BILL. Leroy is a graduate of Hofstra University with a Bachelor of Business Administration degree. He's married to Audrey and they are the proud parents of two daughters.

Leroy has been honored many times in his professional, military and volunteer careers. Two of his most loved honors are being appointed to Account Executive at 3M and Developing a Leadership Program for At Risk High School Students...Chief Encouragement Officer of Self.

www.ReshardConsulting.com

* * * * *

Mark Heilshorn is the co-founder of SpearPoint Solutions. He has had many other roles over the years. First and foremost, he is the father of three - William, Margaret and Henry. He is also the Reverend Dr. Mark Heilshorn, having served congregations in both New Hampshire and Connecticut. In the last 9 years, Mark has served as a salesman and executive for a Medical Transcription company, a revenue cycle solutions company and worked with a National Sales Director for a renowned motivational speaker.

Among Mark's many gifts are his ability to communicate, listen, and inspire the lives of those he encounters. He engenders trust and has a profound love of God and guiding people spiritually and emotionally. Consequently, he has been involved with SpearPoint

Solutions on multiple levels as we define the best ways to empower idea generation.

www.SpearPointOnline.com

www.WhatsTheBIGIdeaGame.com

www.MeaningfulCompany.online

* * * * *

Linda Strother was born in Florida but grew up in N.E. Kentucky, and spent the last 35 years in Tennessee and North Carolina. Linda currently resides in Oxford, NC. She has two grown children; a son and daughter. Retired from the Computer Science Dept. at University of North Carolina at Asheville, she is a huge *Doctor Who* fan and self-confessed geek. She loves to work in her garden, write short stories and create tasty recipes for diabetics.

Currently, Linda is re-inventing her online presence. You can find her blog at TheDiabeticcookbook.net as well as BeckLeeCottageDesigns.com. She's also has a presence on Facebook, Twitter, YouTube & LinkedIn.

Linda has previously published three children's books about *The Adventures of Manni the Long Tailed Raccoon* and *Top Ten Tasty Recipes for Diabetic Diets*.

I was encouraged to write about abundance in health by my friend Isabella and a big thank you to Bob Sager for inviting me to participate in this fantastic abundance project.

www.BeckLeeCottageDesigns.com

* * * * *

Neville Gaunt had a long career as a finance professional in publically listed companies at strategic and operational levels. He is experienced internationally from working in the oil and gas industry, dealing with governments, large and small businesses and complex supply chains. He has negotiated the business maze of short and long-term commercial, political and environmental forces that influence all decisions.

Since choosing to leave corporate life he has been fascinated by leadership and personal and organisational performance. He leads a small team that help organisations permanently improve performance and with the by-product of transforming people's lives. He's involved in a number of social projects helping the homeless, unemployed and improving young people's employability.

Neville is the co-author of two books on leadership and golf, one for adults and one for kids. His favourite saying from Henry Ford *"If you think you can or you think you can't, you're right!"* is why his team focuses on attitude change, and as he says, "then the rest simply falls into place." His aim is to help every young person in every village be Mind Fit - develop a Can-Do attitude with a winning mind.

Neville lives in London, United Kingdom.

www.MindFitLtd.com

* * * * *

Coach **Andy Olds** is entering his 33rd year in both education and coaching. He did his undergraduate work at Capital University in Columbus, Ohio where he played football and coached baseball. He went on to earn his Masters Degree in Sports Science from Indiana University in Bloomington while teaching and coaching baseball for the university.

Andy is currently employed by the Kings Local School District where teaches Physical Education at the Junior High level and also has been serving as the head football coach for the past 19 seasons. In addition, he has also been the Director of Camp Operations for The Anthony Munoz Foundation for 15 years, and has served as the National Director of the NFL's Play 60 Character Camps of the since 2013.

Coach Olds has been married to Pam for almost 30 years and they make their home in Maineville, Ohio. Andy and Pam are parents to sons Tyler and Michael and have one grandchild, Kaylee.

* * * * *

Lisa Baird Panos is a Certified Martha Beck Life Coach who empowers people to create what they crave by helping them rewrite old, untrue stories they tell themselves and transform them into soul-on-fire, inspirational narratives. By helping both men and women break the "Dead End Cycle" of Dream-Excuse-Dream, Lisa uncovers what has kept them stuck and unhappy in their lives and nudges them towards truly listening to their intuition and not their excuses.

Her fresh approach and irreverent style – along with her belief that nothing is impossible – has inspired countless people to redesign and live more meaningful, energizing and fulfilling lives. After navigating her own way through the hardships of parenting, divorce, entrepreneurship, blended families, financial struggles and more – Lisa is now sharing all of her secrets.

Lisa recently released her first book, *Big Girl Pants,* and is currently speaking to a variety of audiences, leading small group workshops and conducting one-on-one coaching sessions with clients across the country.

The mother of two daughters, Lisa currently lives in her hometown of Upper Arlington, Ohio.

www.LisaPanos.com

* * * * *

Tyler Cerny was born in Cleveland, Ohio. He is a recent grad of John Carroll University. During a 4-month study-abroad trip in Beijing, China, Tyler discovered that he loved to travel. One day after his college graduation ceremony, he took a leap of faith and courage and moved to Thailand indefinitely, where he is slowly building an entrepreneurial empire. He is currently a digital marketer focusing on Facebook and Google ads.

Tyler was obese as a kid, weighing 165.7 as a 9-year-old. Since then he has made a total transformation. He's been lifting for 7+ years, played collegiate football, and continues to eat healthy to pursue a fit & active lifestyle. He started a company called Fitness Native which helps gym owners generate more leads through digital marketing.

Fitness Native is a company that uses his skills in marketing and aligns with a passion for fitness and healthy eating.

During his free time, he likes to hike mountains, read and exercise.

www.FitnessNative.com

* * * * *

Teresa Cristina Holden, M.A., is a motivational writer and speaker who uses writing as a creative outlet to influence people to stay inspired and keep the momentum alive in their everyday lives.

She pours her profound knowledge of people and life into her custom made inspirational quotes. She also encourages and uplifts individuals to take the steering wheel of their life with passion and purpose.

Teresa Cristina earned her Master of Arts degree in philosophy and history from the University of Toronto. She had a successful career in education as a professor yet realized that motivational writing was her true passion. Her subject matter includes finding purpose, following your passion, self-love, courage, and leadership in both a personal and professional context. Her words connect with the human spirit and soul. Her philosophical work is current, relevant, intriguing and sought after by professionals in a cross-section of industries.

Using intuition, intimate observation of people and a unique set of experiences, Teresa Cristina is now making waves as a leader in her field. Follow her on tcristina.tv, and on her soon to launch video series.

Teresa Cristina lives with her loving husband and soul-mate Ryan, and beautiful children in Ontario, Canada. Her favorite saying is, "Stay Inspired. Stay blessed!"

* * * * *

Kal Patel is an entrepreneur, consultant and coach. Currently the President/CEO of both 1st Inspection Services and Crestpoint Companies, Kal began his career in the T- shirt business in Colorado.

His road to success included many major setbacks including car accidents, work injuries, financial loss, and several relocations. However, his passion, grit and the support given to him by loyal family and friends he kept along the way helped him to achieve his personal and professional goals.

His experience includes starting up companies on a shoestring budget to exiting with huge financial successes. Kal also is an assistant coach for his daughters jump rope team and spends time by volunteering on several boards/committees as he strongly believes in "paying it forward." He has been happily married for 20 years to his amazingly supportive wife.

www.CrestpointCo.com

* * * * *

Anne Skinner is a Transformational & Executive Coach, Mentor, Speaker, Trainer & 4-time Contributing Author. Anne brings to her clients and her work, 28+ years' experience as a Corporate Sales & Marketing Executive, Leader, Consultant, Entrepreneur, Mentor and Coach, she is a licensed Insurance agent, Real Estate Agent and a Financial Advisor. Anne works with organizations and individuals to facilitate the discovery of the greatness within, then develop themselves and the leadership and financial strategy and skills necessary to transform to new levels in all areas of their lives, careers and relationships.

Anne's passion for empowering individuals, families and organizations, assisting them in creating real and lasting results to live an intentional life of significance and purpose for themselves and their families, comes from her 25 years as a sole support single parent. Her dedication to do all that she can to help others grow into their best version of themselves and navigate life's twists and turns as gracefully and abundantly as possible.

Anne's experiences, lessons and journey have led her to her Dream of a "Fulfilling Life" helping others to navigate and empower themselves to stand in their truth expand and grow. With a wealth of life and professional experience Anne works with those looking to grow and take their life to the next level through 12-month group empowerment mentoring program, life assessment and transformation blueprint program, coaching, mentoring, workshops and speaking engagements.

Anne is currently writing her newest book on *From Surviving to Thriving* to help those in any type of transition to understand the journey ahead, do the necessary inner and outer work, learn new skills to go from surviving to thriving and strategically plan their current and long term life and financial goals to get on track for a fulfilling and prosperous life and retirement.

A Coach, Mentor, Speaker and Trainer, Internationally Certified in Empowerment Mentoring, Assertiveness, Transformation, John Maxwell Leadership and Youth development, Anne has studied with many of the great thought leaders of our time, building her skill and intuition to help transform the lives of many, in all walks of life and all ages.

www.AnneSkinner.net

* * * * *

Ryan Nicley has spent 24 years working as an IT professional in the beauty and wellness industry. His broad experience includes IT, operations, distribution, retail point of sale, customer service, web design, social marketing and the list goes on. His passion and whatever-it-takes mentality has afforded him many experiences and learning opportunities over the year.

Early in his career, and when he was single, he was considered by many to be a "workaholic". Working long hours and traveling consumed much of his time. This was by choice, of course and there was a time when work was all that mattered, or seemed to matter. That began to change when he got married in his early 30's. His wife started to show him the importance of balancing work and personal life. After all, not being single anymore, he was not the only one affected by the long hours and travel. Although reluctant at first, he did begin to see the importance in achieving that balance and started to realize he actually performed better in both work and life when he maintained balance.

Now a father of two children (Addi & Jack), Ryan fully understands the importance balance and believes wholeheartedly in it. He still works hard and sometimes long hours, but he also plays hard and is a very active father and husband.

Ryan loves adventure and the outdoors and puts a lot of emphasize on building memories and sharing experiences with his family. "Our experiences and memories are part of what shapes our lives and I want to create as many as I can with my family."

www.SimpleTechLLC.com

* * * * *

James Savage was born outside of Boston, raised outside of York, PA, and went to high school in Cincinnati, OH. James graduated from the University of Cincinnati with a Communication Theory degree. Two days after graduation, James moved to Lexington, KY to helped start Savage Syndications, a Demand Generation company. Over the past ten years, James and his team has helped many companies grow and expand through their methods, specifically calling campaigns.

Given that the core function of the business is to help build the relationship between clients and their prospects, James has become a master in relationship building, connecting contacts in his network, and helping companies get over their humps no matter what size they are.

James now lives in West Chester, OH. He continues to grow his business, builds amazing networks within the business community around the world, and watches his family grow.

www.SavageDemand.com

* * * * *

From a major loss early in life **Allen (Big Daddy) Walker** has shown endurance and the never-give-up attitude to overcome major disasters and losses in a life filled with constant change.

Allen has trained numerous DJ's, sales people and marketing managers. He is one of the top relationship marketing specialists in the country. Training his staff and thousands of others in the art of customer experience, Allen brings an uplifting positive message that is sure to help you make the life changes you need to make it to that next level.

www.BigDaddyWalkerProductions.com

* * * * *

Charlie Cottrelle is an 18-year-old entrepreneur from Toronto, Ontario. After graduating from Upper Canada College in 2016 he moved on to pursue his Bachelor of Commerce at Queen's Smith School for Business where he and his team operate their career-centered video resume company.

In addition to his role as a contributing author, Charlie is working as a sales associate at a Canadian marketing firm. He also manages his own business and co-leads customer acquisition at a Toronto-based start-up firm.

After noticing a lack of talented students in the Canadian workforce, Charlie has made it his goal to help as many students find work as he possibly can.

Jeffrey Misner is a charismatic young man who has always loved helping people. He has demonstrated his mentoring abilities through multiple leadership roles at his high school.

As a member of the board of stewards and captain of the football and rugby teams, Jeff aided members of the school community through any means possible. Tutoring, Interview prepping, and supplying summer jobs were only a few of the projects that Jeff prided himself in.

Now, he has directed his spirit of entrepreneurship into multiple ventures. He is currently running or in the process of orchestrating businesses in the fashion, fin-tech, drop shipping and machine-learning marketing industries. With this venture, Jeff intends to completely makeover candidate's CV and job-hunting profiles. He wants to help students understand their strengths and the value they can bring to the workforce.

* * * * *

Randall C. Daniels has over 25 years of consistent success in Sales, Management and Personal Development. His Record Breaking sales success has been a constant in a variety of industries including B2B, IT Solutions, Auto Industry, Franchising, Education and Retail. As an unyielding competitor, his top performances have left his mark on many walls and record books.

Randall is a high-quality speaker with the ability to ignite fire within every individual he touches and motivate people toward peak performance. His approach is dynamic, exciting and interactive. His goal when he speaks is to provide immediate improvement followed by long-term positive results.

Randall now trains on effective sales and marketing. He has a passion to help others succeed and live the life of their dreams. He believes that everyone can sell their product or service once they are equipped with the tools and confidence to succeed. He attributes much of his success to working for great companies that believed in the development of people. Throughout his years in sales he's been blessed to receive world class training internationally and domestically.

Unknowingly embarking upon a sales journey in 1979, Randall learned the value of training. Given some instructional tapes to view he took notes and he believed. He quickly outpaced his seasoned peers and received a managerial promotion while just a junior in high school. Belief in training and instruction was already rooted in Randall because of his success growing up as a winning athlete and chess player. While serving in the military Randall traveled around the US and Europe on the army boxing team and basketball team. Training and instruction in sports taught him to compete against himself daily to improve upon all facets of his life and strive to be the best. He kept that competitive drive, determination and work ethic as a professional and has left a trail of sales records along the way.

Randall has an extensive list of Sales Training Program credentials: NEE, MSS, CIWSS, PCS, CCSP but he believes what's most important is leaving an impact. He believes, if you foster new thinking with an objective mind set. You can transform busyness into productiveness, by identifying the best use of time and talent. You can have dramatic improvement in productivity with minor improvement in skills.

* * * * *

Devamalya De (Dev) helps companies fulfill their project and service delivery targets. A Civil Engineer with Masters in Construction Management and Business Administration, Dev has executed key real estate projects as senior resource in Mumbai, India for premium developers; lead startups and handled P&L for Consultants. Currently heading Engineering & Project Management verticals of a renowned Contracting firm in the GCC, implementing best & next practices across the Holding companies.

Dev's interests stretch from the latest developments in management and technology, creative writing, workshops, non-dualistic meditation, travelling, photography and adventure sports. A certified Bullet Proof Manager, he has advanced certifications in Project Management, Quantity Surveying and Planning softwares. He believes in lifelong learning and nothing keeps him more alive and kicking than learning some new stuff. In the past one year, he has learnt the ropes of 3d printing, arduino, micro-drone making and wants to keep adding to the list.

Dev believes life can't be planned and success comes to those who can jump off the cliff and build a plane on the way down.

He splits his time between Mumbai and GCC, has a wife who is a classical Indian dancer cum homemaker and they are blessed with a son aged six.

* * * * *

Angie Grimes, also known as Muse Maven, has had a life of ups and downs. She's had career successes as well as career confusion and failure. Getting to the other side of, debt, relationship issues, divorce, death, parenting and health challenges (including depression) have taught her many life lessons that she is inspired to share.

A serial entrepreneur with a passion for startups, she's experienced many highs and lows, in career and life. She recently embarked on a more heart-centered path. Her focus now is to teach others to look within and awaken. She guides individuals using practical techniques to reactivate spiritual connection so they can begin masterfully building the life of their desires.

Angie was born in Wyoming, spent most of her childhood throughout the West Coast & currently resides in Dallas, TX. Never having wanted children, she unexpectedly found herself a new mother and it has changed her in ways she would never have imagined. When she had her son she made a vow when that she would love, nurture, support him and provide just enough dysfunction to make him funny.

www.Angie-Grimes.com

* * * * *

Don Skaggs is an inventor, entrepreneur, speaker, author & consultant. He is President of the Inventors Network KY and EmpoweredInventing.com. His experience includes bootstrapping startup companies from initial idea to successful exit, developing products and marketing strategies, and successfully launching new products. The Inventors Network KY is a nonprofit that helps inventors and entrepreneurs through education and support services. In addition to his work at the Inventors Network KY, Don also conducts a myriad of speaking engagements - including one to a national audience at the Engadget Expand conference in NYC. In 2016, he launched Empowered Inventing, a program that provides educational, in-depth training and tools for inventors & entrepreneurs.

In his 20+ years of experience, he has bootstrapped companies from startup to exit, negotiated with multinational companies, developed product lines, orchestrated product launches, negotiated company acquisitions, introduced new technologies to untapped markets, and has created and launched national conferences and events. In 1991, he co-founded US Biotex Corporation, successfully developing and introducing many new innovations into the pathology laboratory market. In 2001 he founded 3Gen Scientific, a specialty product developer for the life-science industry. He holds a CBA at Gatton College of Business and Economics, along with several patents and patents pending.

www.EmpoweredInventing.com

* * * * *

Eartha Watts-Hicks is the founder of Earthatone Publishing and Earthatone Books. Former director of publications for Cultivating Our Sisterhood International Association (COSIA), she is a member of the American Society of Composers and Authors and Publishers (ASCAP), and the legendary Harlem Writers Guild.

A fiction fellow of the Hurston/Wright Foundation, Center for Black Literature and North Country Institute and Retreat for Writers of Color, Eartha's writings have appeared in several online publications, including *Harlem World Magazine,* TheUrbanBookSource.com, and Future Executives.org.

Her writing advice has been featured in The Writer's Guide to 2013. In June of 2013, she received the Just R.E.A.D. "Game Changer" Award in the fiction category from the NYCHA branch of the NAACP and was named New York City literacy ambassador. In 2014, she was featured in the Congressional Black Caucus as part of the Write It Down panel discussion.

A PR writer and affiliate of BlackPR.com, she specializes in press releases for entrepreneurs, ministries, and nonprofits. She also leads writing, self-publishing, and publicity workshops for the New York Public Library, The National Writers Union, and The New York City Parks Department. Eartha is currently editor-in-chief at *Harlem World Magazine.*

www.EarthaTone.com

* * * * *

Scott Taylor grew up in Southern California where he started working as a handyman at age 12, becoming foreman at age 16 and starting his first business in construction. At 19 he served a mission for two years in Ireland. There he was shot at, frisked and interrogated by the I.R.A.; but many of his most cherished life experiences occurred there. Upon his return to the U.S. he was married and had three children, eventually settling in Southern Utah. There he wrote his first book *The Opportunity in Every Problem.*

Scott has also spent time living in England and hiking around Western Europe; ultimately coming back to the U.S. where he lives with his wife in Fort Worth Texas. Wherever his adventures have taken him, he's spent most of his professional life as an owner or Director of Sales and marketing. He is currently the Sales and Marketing Director at Cloudia Assistant; a CRM and Marketing system.

Humbled by the ability to mentor, Scott's enriching life experiences have helped him be a positive influence to prisoners, the downtrodden and those seeking a better opportunity in life.

www.CloudiaAssistant.com

* * * * *

Raul Socha grew up in Colombia (South America) and arrived in the United States at the age of 19 with limited language skills; he persevered in the journey of learning, and getting ahead in life. He eventually made his way through higher education to earn a graduate degree, and continue his Trek of Purpose in being a man of faith, husband, father, servant, and leader.

He is passionate about helping individuals and businesses manage everyday risk. Raul has served on numerous boards, volunteered with many non-profit organizations, has helped several businesses generate profitable growth and has authored articles and case studies. He has been a guest speaker at several places in the subject of risk management, insurance, faith, and business.

Raul lives in Worcester, Massachusetts with his beloved wife, Mayra, and their dog, Lolita Marcela.

* * * * *

Alan L. (Al) Lindeman has an extensive and diverse background. Professionally, Al has over 30 years of experience in the Facility Services, Energy Services, and Mechanical Contracting industries.

During those 30 years he worked for Honeywell, ADT Security Systems, and Perfection Group, Inc. He held positions ranging from sales rep, sales manager, general manager, and vice president. In every position, Al worked closely and successfully with all aspects of the companies he worked for – sales, operations, administration, and management.

During those years Al developed a real passion for learning, and as a result, he studied extensively and regularly attended a wide variety of seminars covering leadership, management, organizational development, personal development, and sales. From his studies, he implemented many of the concepts he had learned - helping his team and company successfully grow revenues and profits. As a result of his studies, combined with his extensive sales and management background, Al developed a number of training programs for the companies he worked for, as well as, for various professional and industry associations. He has taught and designed a variety of leadership, management and sales related programs. It was through delivering and attending these programs that he realized what his true professional passion is - training, coaching and mentoring.

In 2012 Al left Perfection Group and with the help of his friend, Tim Burgess, started a training and consulting firm, the Compass Development Group LLC. Since starting Compass they have worked with a variety of companies and organizations (e.g. Proctor & Gamble, USI Insurance, Quality Gold, and others) to help them maximize their results through leadership, organizational development, as well as sales and sales leadership.

In 2014 Al and Tim decided to take the sales and leadership expertise and blend it with Tim's 15 years of very successful real estate sales to form a second company called Maximizing Results LLC. Under the Maximizing Result umbrella, Al and Tim offer training, coaching, and mentoring programs for organizations and individuals. They are serving a client base that currently spreads across the United States, and are also starting to attract an international following. The programs and services offered through Maximizing Results are providing clients with significant improvements in their professional and personal lives.

Al truly has a passion for life and for helping others. As his company's by-line states "Maximizing Results In Business and Life" Al wants to help the organizations and individuals that he works with to become the very best version of themselves personally and professionally. Through the training and coaching programs offered, he is making a positive difference in people's lives.

www.MaximizingResultsLLC.com

* * * * *

Michelle Sager was born in Kentucky but has lived mostly in Ohio, with a short, relaxing hiatus from winter in East Tennessee. She attended McAuley High School and Bowling Green State University. Married for twenty-one years, Michelle is a mother to 2 homeschooled children, step-mother to 2 adult children and grandmother to 1, so far. She is passionate about volunteering, and her current beneficiary is Girl Scouts.

Prior to being a stay-at-home and home schooling Mom, she worked with Procter and Gamble in Global Product Standards. Michelle is an Author, Teacher, Book Editor and Creator of Home Schooling curriculums. Talented at organizing, she is now the Operations Manager for SpearPoint Solutions.

* * * * *

Yvette Adams is a married and a homeschooling mother of 5 children (26,23,20,17 and 1). After growing up in New York City, she now lives in Blythewood, South Carolina.

After spending years working as an auditor, Yvette has made her living in the financial services industry for the last 10 years. She is a representative with World Financial Group and helps individual and business clients with protection plans and long term financial planning.

* * * * *

Bob Sager was born in Iowa, but has lived in Ohio most of his life. The Founder of SpearPoint Solutions, Bob's professional background includes work in the Real Estate business and in Financial Planning. The curator of and contributing author to *Living a Wealthy Life*, Bob is also the inventor of an innovative thinking game and app called What's The BIG Idea? and the Author of a personal achievement book, *Discovering Your Greatness.* He believes strongly in the power of collaboration and coaching which led him to create a conference call based business networking, idea creation and coaching entity called Meaningful Connections.

When his time is not occupied with professional pursuits, Bob enjoys playing and listening to music, playing golf and reading. Bob also enjoys watching a wide variety of sports; most avidly NFL football. He is married to Michelle, has 4 children, ages 30 -17, and is proud to be called Grandpa.

www.SpearPointOnline.com

www.WhatsTheBIGIdeaGame.com

www.MeaningfulCompany.online

Made in the USA
Lexington, KY
17 November 2017